SMART MEAL PREP FOR BEGINNERS

SMART
MEAL
PREP
for Beginners

RECIPES AND WEEKLY PLANS
FOR HEALTHY, READY-TO-GO MEALS

Toby Amidor, MS, RD, CDN

PHOTOGRAPHY BY ELYSA WEITALA

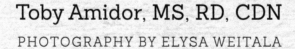

R

ROCKRIDGE
PRESS

Designers: Katy Brown and Will Mack
Editor: Stacy Wagner-Kinnear
Production Editor: Andrew Yackira
Photography © Elysa Weitala, 2018; Styling by Alexa Hyman
Author photo © Melani Lust Photography

ISBN: Print 978-1-64152-125-3 | eBook 978-1-64152-126-0

To my three most precious gifts
in my life: my children,
Schoen, Ellena, and Micah.
I love you.

Contents

GRAINS & VEGETABLE SIDES 139

SNACKS 151

Introduction

IS THERE ANYONE WHO *ISN'T* BUSY? For pretty much all of us, time is precious. I'm a mother of three kids. I run the household, work full-time, and often find myself shuttling the kids to school and activities. For years, getting healthy meals on the table was no easy feat. Before I got into the meal prepping groove, I spent too much time each day cooking, I was saddled with high food bills, and I watched a lot of food go to waste.

Since those days, I've learned that spending a few hours over the weekend planning meals, food shopping, and cooking is an incredible timesaver. I've been able to free myself of unnecessary stress, spend more time with my kids, reduce my grocery bill, and even find time to hit my favorite evening Pilates class. But there was a learning curve.

When I first started meal prepping, I didn't always want to spend time cooking during my precious weekend. I found it challenging to balance weekend activities with the planning and prepping of numerous meals. To make it more manageable, I started preparing only two or three meals and gradually worked my way up to about six. Some weekends I would cook three dishes, while on others I could prep six dishes, depending on my schedule. These days, sometimes I prep a double batch of certain dishes (like lasagna, meatballs, or soup), and freeze half for those weeks when I don't have time to prep. I've learned to build up my stash of frozen meals and balance it with just a few dishes I prep on Sunday—that's what I call *smart* meal prepping.

As a registered dietitian, I know that eating healthy is challenging. I wrote my first meal prep guide, *The Healthy Meal Prep Cookbook*, to show people just how easy it can be to prepare nutritious, ready-to-eat, portion-controlled meals. But I've come to realize that many people don't just want general guidance; they want specific, step-by-step instructions and meal prep plans that tell them what to eat and for which meal. While you're always welcome to tweak recipes and preps as you desire, this book was written to make sure you never have to do any guesswork as you begin to meal prep. Follow the cooking and storing instructions, eat the meals on the days specified, and you'll succeed. It's as easy as that.

In this cookbook, I provide six weeks of progressive meal prep plans. The first two plans have you prepare just three recipes for the week, to ease you in. The final meal prep plan gives you six recipes. You can also gauge your individual needs and decide how many recipes you'll want to prepare for any given week. Whatever you choose, your end result will be a less stressful life filled with delicious, healthy, and *ready* meals.

PART ONE

MEAL PREP MADE EASY

SMART MEAL PREP

SIMPLY PUT, MEAL PREP is the act of preparing and storing in advance several individual servings of one or more weekly meals and snacks. Although meal planning is involved, meal prep takes the selection and scheduling of meals a step further by actually having them fully cooked and boxed. Meal prepping can be done one or two days each week, depending on your individual needs and schedule. The same meal will be divided and boxed for several meals throughout the week and be ready to heat-and-eat, like a casserole, or eat cold, like a salad. But the benefits of meal prepping go a lot further than just convenience.

Meal Prep Benefits

Meal prepping changed my life. The most meaningful benefit for me was that it empowered me to feed my family healthy, flavorful meals every day. But there are so many more reasons to meal prep:

Save money. Meal prepping allows you to plan every meal with recipes that repurpose numerous ingredients. You'll also know the exact amount to buy of expensive foods like meat, fish, and poultry, which helps minimize grocery bills (and waste).

Save time. When you spend some time one or two days each week preparing the meals in this book, you'll shave off the time you'd otherwise spend prepping on busy weeknights. If you're stuck late at work, want to work out, or just want to enjoy more quality time with your family, smart meal prepping allows you to do it.

Eat healthier. Each week you'll select healthy, easy recipes to prepare and have at your fingertips. This can help minimize those desperation pit stops at fast-food joints or the donut shop when hunger takes over and there's nothing ready to eat in the house.

Control your weight. With weight loss or weight maintenance, keeping portions in check is one of the biggest hurdles to overcome. Every week, you'll box each meal, which is an awesome tool for managing food portions.

Improve multitasking skills. When cooking several recipes on one day, you'll be multitasking. For example, you may be roasting vegetables while the slow cooker is running, and simultaneously slicing fruit for a breakfast parfait. In this book, it's all laid out in a straightforward and manageable way.

Decrease stress. I get it—cooking every night is extremely stressful. You need to choose a recipe or recipes to cook, have all the ingredients available, cook the dish or dishes, serve the meal, and clean up. With smart meal prepping, you skip right over these steps without worrying "what's for dinner?" every single night.

Get more done with less effort. One trick with meal prepping is to cook a double batch and freeze half for a later date. It takes substantially less effort to cook extra muffins or chili than it does to cook a new recipe every night of the week, so take advantage!

MEAL PREP DOS AND DON'TS

Developing smart meal prepping habits is part of the learning process. Here are some meal prep dos and don'ts worth keeping in mind as you get started:

✔ **DO flag healthy recipes you love.** After trying healthy recipes, keep the ones you love in a folder or mark them in the cookbook.

✔ **DO go at your own pace.** You can successfully meal prep with three recipes or six recipes. You don't need to prepare 10 or more recipes for the week. Start slowly and build your way up.

✔ **DO work with your schedule.** Some weeks you'll be able to prepare more recipes than other weeks. Do whatever works for you and your schedule.

✔ **DO freeze extras.** Some weeks you will have a few extra meals. Freezer-friendly meals can be frozen and kept for up to a few months, as noted in the recipes.

✔ **DO make cleanup easy.** You'll have many vegetable scraps, eggshells, and empty containers to toss, so keep your recycling, compost bin, and trash nearby for easy cleanup.

✗ **DON'T leave everything until the last minute.** Plan ahead for best results. Meal prepping is about scheduling your time in advance, so you can get to the market and buy the ingredients you need, then spend the necessary time at home preparing them.

✗ **DON'T divide meals later.** The last step of meal prepping is to divide recipes into individual portions and pack them into containers. Don't skip this step or divide meals right before digging into one. Dividing meals up front helps maintain good portion control, prevents last-minute scrambling to divide meals, and ensures your meals will last through the week.

✗ **DON'T overprep.** The last thing you want to do is prep meals that will go uneaten, unless of course you can freeze them. To get into the meal prepping jive, start slow and get to know your meal prepping needs. You can meal prep one or two days a week—do whatever works with your schedule.

Meal Prep in 5 Steps

For successful meal prepping, I recommend following these five steps:

1. CHOOSE WHEN TO PREP

Select one or two days to meal prep. Sundays work best for many folks, but another day during the week might work better for you. For example, if you work over the weekend, then a day off during the week is probably a better day for you to meal prep. You can also choose two days each week to prep food. Because my kids have so many activities over the weekend, it's tough for me to prep five or six recipes at a time. So I do my meal prepping over the course of a few hours on Sundays and Wednesdays.

2. DECIDE WHICH MEALS TO PREP

This cookbook lays out which foods to prep each week. There are six (one-week) meal prep plans, which range from three recipes to six recipes. They don't need to be done in the order written. For example, you can start with Prep 1, do the same prep for a few weeks, and then jump to Prep 4 the following week. It all depends on the time you have, how many recipes you'd like to make each week, and which meals sound good to you. Once you've tried all six weeks, you may want to repeat some preps, or add a bit of variety. You can swap out one or several recipes from part 2 of this cookbook.

When deciding which recipes to swap into your meal prep schedule, keep variety in mind when it comes to protein, whole grains, and veggies. Nutritionally, this will allow you to take in a wider range of nutrients. If one meal for the week is fish with asparagus, you'll probably want to select a chicken, beef, pork, or vegetarian recipe with a different vegetable to rotate with during the week. At the same time, try to keep some of the ingredients between recipes the same, which can help decrease food costs and help use up an ingredient. For example, if you have broccoli in an egg dish for breakfast, plan to use up the remaining broccoli as a side for one of the lunch or dinner meals.

When you're in the groove and feeling comfortable with the meal prep process, you can also create and customize your own meal prep plans using the extra recipes in part 2. Here are two different examples of pairing meals:

WEIGHT LOSS PREP FOR WOMEN

If you're a woman whose goal is to lose weight and take in 1,300 calories per day, try combining these recipes (note that every individual has different caloric needs for weight loss, but this is an average):

- Veggie Delight Breakfast Egg Casserole (page 107)
- Chicken Pad Thai over Zucchini Noodles (page 129)
- Lemon-Caper Tilapia with Whole-Wheat Couscous (page 120)
- Sunflower Power Bites (page 160)

FLEXITARIAN PREP

If you're not ready to go vegetarian or vegan for a week but do want to eat more of a plant-based diet, try this combination:

- Peanut Butter–Banana Oatmeal (page 104)
- Slow Cooker Two-Bean Sloppy Joes (page 113)
- Lemon-Caper Tilapia with Whole-Wheat Couscous (page 120)
- Nutty Trail Mix (page 156)

3. GO FOOD SHOPPING

To make the most of your time and money, after selecting your recipes, go through the ingredients and check if you have them. List the ingredients you need to purchase according to the flow of your market. For example, if you shop at a traditional supermarket, produce is usually the first place you'll find yourself. I typically categorize my shopping list in this order: fruits, vegetables and herbs, milk and dairy, proteins (like meat, chicken, and fish), packaged goods, and frozen items. Note how much you need of each ingredient to avoid buying too much. But don't worry about this straight away. For this book's meal preps, the shopping lists specify the amount of each ingredient you'll need.

One note of caution about recipes with the gluten-free designation: Some ingredients, oats for example, are sometimes processed in facilities that also handle foods that contain gluten. If avoiding gluten is important to you, always check package labels carefully to make sure the ingredient is gluten-free.

GO-TO INGREDIENTS

A key to smart meal prepping is using the same ingredients for several meals. For example, quinoa is a staple in my house, and I can use it to serve with a stir-fry or as a side to fish. The specific ingredients you'll see used repeatedly in this book are easy to find, affordable, and able to be stored in the refrigerator, freezer, or pantry. Don't forget that all meals should have a good balance of whole grain, lean protein, and lots of veggies so you take in the wide variety of nutrients your body needs to stay healthy. Think of snacks as mini meals to round out your balanced diet, and remember that these should include fruits, dairy, whole grains, and yes, more veggies.

The following are my go-to ingredients that I use in this cookbook:

Vegetables
- Asparagus
- Broccoli
- Carrots
- Cauliflower
- Celery
- Onions
- Portobello mushrooms
- Russet potatoes
- Spinach
- Sweet potatoes
- Tomatoes
- Zucchini

Lean Protein
- Beans (black, pinto)
- Chicken breast, skinless, boneless
- Eggs
- Ground beef (at least 90% lean)

- Lentils
- Nuts (cashews, almonds, pecans)
- Peanut butter
- Salmon

Whole Grains
- Brown rice
- Farro
- Oats
- Quinoa
- Sorghum
- Whole-grain pasta
- Whole-wheat couscous

Fruits
- Bananas
- Berries (strawberries, blueberries)
- Melon
- Pineapple

Dairy
- Milk, nonfat or low-fat (1%)
- Mozzarella cheese, part-skim
- Parmesan cheese, grated
- Yogurt, Greek, nonfat plain and vanilla

Healthy Fats
- Canola oil
- Olive oil
- Nonstick cooking oil spray

A smart prep day is an efficient one. For each of the weekly preps, I provide the order in which recipes should be cooked and when to start each recipe, to take out the guesswork.

In general, this is a good rule of thumb for meal prep order:

- Always start with the slow cooker recipe (if applicable).
- Prep ingredients, such as vegetables and proteins, for recipes that take longer to cook, so you can get those recipes started.
- Prep sauces and dressings that may be needed. For example, if the chicken needs to be marinated (which takes at least 30 minutes), prepare the marinade earlier in your meal prep day so you can start marinating right away.
- Begin longer-cooking recipes, especially recipes that will be baked or roasted in the oven or stove top for over 20 minutes. Once these dishes are cooking, you can continue prepping other recipes.
- Prep nuts and fruit.
- Leave shorter recipes for down-times. Easy no-cook recipes (like To-Go Peanut Butter–Veggie Jars, page 153) can be prepared when you're waiting for a recipe to finish cooking in the oven or simmering on the stove top.
- Cook the remaining recipes, which should be easier since you've already prepped most of the ingredients.
- Portion and pack meals and snacks into single-serve containers. Stack in your refrigerator or pantry (if applicable) so they're grab-and-go-ready. Extra meals that are freezer-friendly can be frozen right away.

The last point of the previous step brings us here. All preps end with portioning and packing so you can easily grab and go. The exact portions (or serving size) for each meal are listed within each recipe. Meals can be packed in several different types of containers (see page 10).

As a rule of thumb, your meal should consist of this combination:

- one-quarter lean protein (typically 3 to 4 ounces of fish, chicken, pork, or beef) or a vegetarian protein source (such as tofu, eggs, beans, or lentils)

- one-quarter whole grains (about ¾ to 1 cup)
- one-half vegetables or fruit (about 1 cup)

If you're going to increase any component of a meal, I recommend upping the veggies or fruit. If you make an all-in-one dish like the Sesame Chicken with Asparagus and Red Peppers (page 128), pair it with a whole grain like Herbed Quinoa (page 140) to balance your plate. Portions vary between dishes, but typically an all-in-one dish should be 1½ to 2 cups per serving (or as indicated in the serving size of the recipes in this book).

For the snacks in this cookbook, you'll typically find dairy, whole grains, fruit, and vegetables in the mix. One serving of dairy can be 1 cup for yogurt and milk, while 1 cup of fruits or vegetables is a good guideline. According to the 2015–2020 Dietary Guidelines for Americans, 90 percent of Americans don't meet the recommended daily amount of vegetables, and 85 percent of Americans don't meet the recommended daily amount of fruit. Again, if you're going to increase a food, fruits and vegetables are your best option.

All the recipes in this cookbook provide the *exact* amounts to pack in a box, which takes the guesswork out of portion control.

Essential Storage Containers

You'll want to have a collection of single-serve storage containers—these are essential for meal prepping. Proper containers help maintain the flavor, color, and texture of stored foods. The right container reduces exposure to air, which also helps maintain the food's quality and makes it last longer throughout the week.

The following are characteristics to look for:

Single compartment or multiple: When it comes to the presentation of food, every person is different. Some folks don't mind when their foods touch each other, while others do. That is when you can select single versus multiple compartment containers. I prefer multiple compartments as I like to enjoy each food separately, but it's a personal decision.

Stackable/nestable: Stackable containers use space wisely so you can maximize space while keeping your food organized for the week. Many such containers can fold or stack nicely when not in use, which means more organized storage cabinets as well.

BPA-free: The industrial chemical bisphenol A (BPA) has been around since the 1960s, but in recent years, the term "BPA-free" has become top of mind to many shoppers. Although the Food and Drug Administration concluded that BPA found in storage containers is safe in small amounts, for frequent use, I recommend selecting BPA-free storage containers. They're easy to find and are indicated as BPA-free on the package. Purchase containers made specifically for food, as opposed to containers that are for storing other nonfood items like office supplies or work bench items. Those containers may contain BPA and are not food-safe. Glass containers do not contain BPA.

Leakproof: The worst days begin when I get to work and realize my grab-and-go container has spilled in my bag. All my hard meal prepping work is rendered useless, and I end up spending more money ordering lunch

FOOD STORAGE GUIDELINES

When storing food in your refrigerator and freezer, it's really important to always label and date the containers. Of course you'll want to rotate and use the earliest dates first to minimize food spoilage. When storing food in the refrigerator, place raw foods at the bottom, wrapped to catch any juices. Ready-to-eat foods like cooked dishes and fresh food like fruits, vegetables, and yogurt should be stored above the raw food. This will help minimize the risk of cross-contamination and potential foodborne illness. It's also important to use foods when they're at their peak of freshness and nutrition. On the following page is a chart illustrating freezer and refrigerator storage times of popular foods.

	FRIDGE	FREEZER
Salads: egg salad, tuna salad, chicken salad, pasta salad	**3 TO 5 DAYS**	**DOES NOT FREEZE WELL**
Hamburger, meatloaf, and other dishes made with ground meat (raw)	**1 TO 2 DAYS**	**3 TO 4 MONTHS**
Steaks: beef, pork, lamb (raw)	**3 TO 5 DAYS**	**3 TO 4 MONTHS**
Chops: beef, pork, lamb (raw)	**3 TO 5 DAYS**	**4 TO 6 MONTHS**
Roasts: beef, pork, lamb (raw)	**3 TO 5 DAYS**	**4 TO 12 MONTHS**
Whole chicken or turkey (raw)	**1 TO 2 DAYS**	**1 YEAR**
Pieces: chicken or turkey (raw)	**1 TO 2 DAYS**	**9 MONTHS**
Soups and stews with vegetables and meat	**3 TO 4 DAYS**	**2 TO 3 MONTHS**
Pizza	**3 TO 4 DAYS**	**1 TO 2 MONTHS**
Beef, lamb, pork, or chicken (cooked)	**3 TO 4 DAYS**	**2 TO 6 MONTHS**

*Chart based on FoodSafety.gov

out that day. Before purchasing containers, do a little research and even some home testing for leaks. If you commute to work by train, bus, or car, test out containers or read reviews that speak to these conditions.

Microwave-, dishwasher-, and freezer-safe: Some of your meals will be reheated in the microwave, while others may be stored in the freezer for another time. As such, I recommend finding containers that can withstand both microwaving and freezing. If you're looking to save a little more time during cleanup and you have a dishwasher, containers that you can pop right in the dishwasher are a smart choice.

My preference is glass mason jars of various sizes (there are even small ones perfect for dressings). When using mason jars to store meals, you'll want to make sure to buy widemouthed jars, or they will be difficult to pack. I also have plastic containers that I love and use regularly for meal prep. But do what works for you in terms of budget, storage, and transport.

6 Weeks of Meal Prep

In this cookbook, you'll find six weeks of meal preps that have been written to produce meals for one person. While I specify breakfast items, I've made a point to include recipes for lunches and dinners that are pretty much inter-changeable, recognizing that oftentimes one night's dinner leftovers become the next day's lunch. Here's the breakdown for each week:

- **Meal prep 1 and 2**: 1 breakfast and 2 lunches

- **Meal prep 3**: 1 breakfast, 3 lunches/dinners

- **Meal prep 4 and 5**: 1 breakfast, 3 lunches/dinners, and 1 snack

- **Meal prep 6**: 2 breakfasts, 3 lunches/dinners, and 1 snack

The meal prep weeks start out with only three recipes, progressing to six recipes. Breakfast and lunch are typically the meals that people spend money on outside of the home during the week. By meal prepping these two meals, you can save between $10 and $15 a day instead (adding up to $50 to $75 dollars in a workweek). It also takes time to become adept at multi-tasking with different recipes in the kitchen and get into the meal-prepping groove. Feel free to repeat preps before moving on, or do them in a different order. Do what you feel comfortable with and what works best with your schedule and available meal prep time.

I've tried my best to make sure nearly all the meals produced are eaten in one week, but sometimes ending up with extra meals was unavoidable. In these cases, I've noted where they can be frozen or served to family members or guests.

Every meal prep chapter includes a meal plan, shopping list, step-by-step prepping and cooking instructions, and the recipes that you'll make that week. Each recipe includes the number of servings, serving size, and nutrition information for calories, total and saturated fat, protein, total carbs, fiber, sugar, and sodium. You'll also find a "Toby's Tip" that will give you my recommendations to make the meal more nutritious, or suggestions on how to modify the dish to your liking.

Smart Prep Is Simple Prep

The purpose of this cookbook is to help you create the healthy habit of meal prepping. As mentioned, it's best to start with the more manageable preps, get a feel for what works for you, and slowly build your way up. Early prep weeks may sacrifice some variety for ease, but never at the expense of flavor.

Being successful early on can empower and motivate you to prep more and to prep a wider variety of dishes. You may have seen gorgeous meal prep photos on the Internet, with promises of 15 dishes prepared in one week. These advanced meal preps shouldn't be attempted right out of the gate, as they can overwhelm and discourage a beginner. Start here with simple recipes that are 100 percent doable, with ingredients that are easy to find. This cookbook was set up for your success in meal prepping, and hopefully it will become the norm in your everyday life and a lifelong healthy habit!

MEAL PREP 1

"START EASY" IS MY MOTTO FOR SUCCESS! The first meal prep is designed to get you in the swing of things. It's also a suitable schedule if you have dinner plans for the weeknights, so you can have breakfast and lunch all set up. If lunches aren't a challenge for you, feel free to consider the "lunch" meals your dinner. The idea here is to do what works for you and your schedule. The protein selection varies throughout the meals, from salmon and eggs to chicken to beef, while the side grains for lunch rotate between brown rice and quinoa. To keep the remaining meals that you eat during the week well balanced, make sure to include at least two more sources of dairy (preferably low-fat or nonfat), fruit, and more vegetables.

« Smoked Salmon Breakfast Bowl (page 20)

SHOPPING LIST

PANTRY

- Balsamic vinegar
- Bay leaves
- Black beans, low-sodium (1 [15-ounce] can)
- Black pepper, freshly ground
- Broth, low-sodium vegetable (4 cups)
- Brown sugar
- Canola oil
- Capers
- Cayenne pepper
- Chili powder
- Cornstarch
- Crackers, whole-grain
- Cumin, ground
- Lentils (1 [15-ounce] can)
- Olive oil
- Paprika
- Quinoa
- Rice, long-grain brown
- Salsa
- Salt
- Soy sauce, low-sodium

FRESH PRODUCE

- Basil (1 bunch)
- Cucumbers, Kirby or Persian (4)
- Garlic (3 cloves)
- Ginger (2-inch piece)
- Lemons (2)
- Mushrooms, brown cremini or baby bella (10 ounces)
- Onions, yellow (2)
- Parsley (1 bunch)
- Peppers, red bell (4)
- Scallions (1 bunch)
- Tomatoes, plum (1 pound)

PROTEIN

- Beef, top sirloin (1 pound)
- Chicken, skinless, boneless breast (6 ounces)
- Eggs, large (5)
- Salmon, smoked (5 ounces)

DAIRY

- Cheese, Monterey Jack or Cheddar (5 ounces)

EQUIPMENT

- Chef's knife
- Cutting board
- Measuring cups and spoons
- Mixing bowls
- Saucepans
- Skillet or wok
- Stockpot

STEP-BY-STEP PREP

Before you begin, keep in mind that the beef for the **Beef and Mushroom Stir-Fry over Brown Rice with Lentils** (page 22) needs to marinate for a minimum of 30 minutes but can marinate for up to 24 hours. If you prefer a longer marinating time, prepare the beef a day before you start the full meal prep.

1.   Begin by preparing the **Brown Rice with Lentils** through step 1 (page 142).

2.   While the rice is cooking, prepare and marinate the beef for the **Beef and Mushroom Stir-Fry over Brown Rice with Lentils** through step 1 (page 22).

	BREAKFAST	LUNCH
DAY 1	Smoked Salmon Breakfast Bowl	Deconstructed Chicken Burritos
DAY 2	Smoked Salmon Breakfast Bowl	Beef and Mushroom Stir-Fry over Brown Rice with Lentils
DAY 3	Smoked Salmon Breakfast Bowl	Deconstructed Chicken Burritos
DAY 4	Smoked Salmon Breakfast Bowl	Beef and Mushroom Stir-Fry over Brown Rice with Lentils
DAY 5	Smoked Salmon Breakfast Bowl	Beef and Mushroom Stir-Fry over Brown Rice with Lentils

3. Once the rice is cooked, fluff it with a fork and finish preparing the **Brown Rice with Lentils** recipe through step 3 (page 142).

4. Prepare the **Herbed Quinoa** through step 1 (page 140) for the **Deconstructed Chicken Burritos** (page 21).

5. While the quinoa is cooking, prepare the **Smoked Salmon Breakfast Bowl** (page 20), package it in 5 individual containers as instructed, and place them in the refrigerator.

6. Finish preparing the **Herbed Quinoa** (page 140) and set aside.

7. Prepare the **Deconstructed Chicken Burritos** through step 2 (page 21). Allow the chicken mixture to cool.

8. Remove the beef from the refrigerator and finish cooking the stir-fry. In each of 4 containers, place about 1 cup of stir-fry alongside ¾ cup of **Brown Rice with Lentils** (page 142), then refrigerate.

9. Finish the chicken burritos by placing half of the cooled chicken mixture on the side in each of 2 containers. Add ¾ cup of **Herbed Quinoa** (page 140) topped with ¼ cup of black beans to the other side. Place ¼ cup of the salsa in two small separate containers, then refrigerate.

SMOKED SALMON BREAKFAST BOWL

MAKES 5 SERVINGS

PREP TIME: 25 minutes   **COOK TIME:** 3 minutes

This breakfast bowl delivers a well-balanced meal with four food groups. No-fuss smoked salmon is packed with protein and omega-3 fats, while the cheese provides protein and calcium, and the eggs contain protein and lutein, which is good for eye health. If that's not enough, the whole-grain crackers provide fiber, and the vegetables offer antioxidants and phytonutrients, natural plant chemicals that help fight and prevent disease.

5 large eggs

5 ounces smoked salmon, divided into 1-inch-thick pieces

5 teaspoons capers, drained

1 lemon, cut into 10 half-moons

5 ounces Monterey Jack or Cheddar cheese, cut into 1-ounce pieces

4 plum tomatoes, sliced

4 Kirby or Persian cucumbers, sliced

2 red bell peppers, sliced

20 whole-grain crackers

1.   Hard-boil the eggs by placing them in a medium pot and covering them with water. Over high heat, bring the water to a boil. Cook the eggs for 3 minutes, then remove the pot from the heat, cover, and let stand for 15 minutes. Drain the water and place the eggs in a bowl of ice until completely cool, about 10 minutes. Peel the eggs and slice lengthwise.

2.   Into each of 5 containers, place 1 piece of smoked salmon, and top with 1 teaspoon of capers and 2 slices of lemon. Next, place 1 ounce of cheese, 1 egg slice, and even amounts of tomatoes, cucumbers, and peppers on the side of the salmon. Add 4 crackers next to the cheese.

Storage: Place airtight containers in the refrigerator for up to 5 days.

> **TOBY'S TIP:** Feel free to use what you have in your refrigerator. Switch up the vegetables for carrots, celery, broccoli, or cauliflower. Swap the cheese for your favorite, and play around with various whole-grain crackers or use mini whole-grain pitas instead.

Per Serving (1 container): Calories: 298; Total Fat: 16g; Saturated Fat: 8g; Protein: 21g; Total Carbs: 17g; Fiber: 3g; Sugar: 6g; Sodium: 734mg

DECONSTRUCTED CHICKEN BURRITOS

MAKES 2 SERVINGS

PREP TIME: 15 minutes   COOK TIME: 15 minutes

Mexican fare is nicely balanced with veggies, whole grains, beans, and protein. But stuffing and reheating a burrito can get messy. As I tend to be a messy cook, I take certain steps to minimize my mess, such as packing the healthy ingredients of a burrito into a simple, organized bowl or container.

1 tablespoon chili powder

2 teaspoons ground cumin

2 teaspoons paprika

½ teaspoon cayenne pepper

¼ teaspoon salt

¼ teaspoon freshly ground black pepper

4 teaspoons olive oil

1 garlic clove, minced

1 small yellow onion, sliced

2 red bell peppers, cut into ½-inch strips

6 ounces skinless, boneless chicken breasts, cut into 1-inch strips

2 servings (1½ cups) Herbed Quinoa (page 140)

½ cup low-sodium canned black beans, rinsed and drained

½ cup jarred salsa

1.   In a small bowl, mix together the chili powder, cumin, paprika, cayenne, salt, and black pepper.

2.   In a medium skillet over medium heat, heat the olive oil. When the oil is shimmering, add the garlic, onion, and peppers and cook until the vegetables soften, about 3 minutes. Add the chicken strips and cook on all sides, about 8 minutes. Add the spices and toss to evenly coat. Continue cooking until the flavors combine, about 2 more minutes. Set the skillet aside to cool.

3.   Into each of 2 containers, place ¾ cup of Herbed Quinoa and top with ¼ cup of black beans. Place half the chicken mixture on the side. Place ¼ cup of salsa in a separate small container to top the bowl after it's reheated.

Storage: Place airtight containers in the refrigerator for up to 5 days. To reheat, microwave uncovered on high for 2 minutes. Once reheated, top with the salsa.

TOBY'S TIP: Swap the quinoa for Brown Rice with Lentils (page 142) and the salsa for my fresh Meal Prep Salsa (page 91).

Per Serving (1 container): Calories: 600; Total Fat: 28g; Saturated Fat: 4g; Protein: 31g; Total Carbs: 57g; Fiber: 14g; Sugar: 10g; Sodium: 873mg

BEEF AND MUSHROOM STIR-FRY OVER BROWN RICE WITH LENTILS

MAKES 4 SERVINGS

PREP TIME: 15 minutes, plus 30 minutes marinating time   COOK TIME: 15 minutes

One of the easiest meal preps to whip up is a stir-fry. Combine a lean protein with vegetables and serve over a whole grain, and you've got a quick, easy, well-balanced meal that can last throughout the week. Note that the beef can marinate for as little as 30 minutes or as long as 24 hours.

3 tablespoons canola oil, divided

1 tablespoon grated fresh ginger

2 tablespoons low-sodium soy sauce

2 tablespoons balsamic vinegar

1 tablespoon cornstarch

1 teaspoon brown sugar

¼ teaspoon freshly ground black pepper

1 pound top sirloin, cut into 1½-inch strips

1 (10-ounce) container baby bella (brown) mushrooms, thinly sliced

4 servings (3 cups) Brown Rice with Lentils (page 142)

1. In a medium bowl, prepare the marinade by whisking together 2 tablespoons of canola oil, the ginger, soy sauce, balsamic vinegar, cornstarch, brown sugar, and pepper. Place the sirloin strips in a large container and toss with half the marinade. Cover and allow the beef to marinate in the refrigerator for at least 30 minutes and up to 24 hours. Cover and refrigerate the remaining marinade.

2. When the beef is done marinating, heat the remaining 1 tablespoon of canola oil in a wok or large skillet over high heat until it is shimmering. Add the beef strips and discard the marinade from the bowl. Cook the beef until browned on all sides, about 8 minutes. Using a slotted spoon, transfer the beef to a clean plate.

3. Add the mushrooms to the wok and cook over medium-high heat until softened, about 3 minutes. Add the cooked beef and the refrigerated marinade, and stir until slightly thickened, about 2 minutes. Set the wok aside to slightly cool.

4. Into each of 4 containers, place about 1 cup of stir-fry alongside ¾ cup of Brown Rice with Lentils.

Storage: Place airtight containers in the refrigerator for up to 1 week. To freeze, place freezer-safe containers in the freezer for up to 2 months. To defrost, refrigerate overnight. To reheat, microwave uncovered on high for 2 minutes.

TOBY'S TIP: Swap out the sirloin for skinless, boneless chicken breast cut into 1-inch strips.

Per Serving (1 container): Calories: 547; Total Fat: 27g; Saturated Fat: 6g; Protein: 33g; Total Carbs: 45g; Fiber: 8g; Sugar: 5g; Sodium: 623mg

MEAL PREP 2

THIS IS ANOTHER LOW-INTENSITY prep with meals for breakfast and lunch only. It's ideal if you're trying to eat less meat, with the protein stars of the plan being Greek yogurt, fish, and eggs. You will end up with one extra serving of the Tomato, Asparagus, Basil Flounder with Herbed Quinoa, which you can freeze, save for a dinner, or serve to a guest. Happy, healthy meal prepping!

« Superfood Salad with Lemon-Balsamic Vinaigrette (page 30)

SHOPPING LIST

PANTRY
- Balsamic vinegar
- Bay leaves
- Black pepper, freshly ground
- Broth, low-sodium vegetable (1 [14.5 ounce] can)
- Brown rice
- Dijon mustard
- Lentils (1 [14.5-ounce] can)
- Maple syrup, 100% pure
- Olive oil
- Olive oil, extra virgin
- Quinoa
- Salt
- Sunflower seeds, roasted and unsalted
- Walnuts

FRUIT, VEGETABLES, HERBS & SPICES
- Asparagus (1 bunch, about 1 pound)
- Baby spinach (5 ounces)
- Basil (1 bunch)
- Blueberries (3 cups fresh or frozen, 1 cup fresh)
- Carrot (1)
- Cherry tomatoes (2 cups)
- Cucumber (1)
- Garlic (1 head)
- Lemons (4)
- Onion (1)
- Parsley (1 bunch)
- Red onion (1 small)
- Scallions (1 bunch)

PROTEIN
- Eggs (2 large)
- Flounder (4 [5-ounce] fillets)

DAIRY
- Greek yogurt, plain nonfat (1 [32-ounce] container)

EQUIPMENT

- Baking sheet
- Chef's knife
- Cutting board
- Measuring cups and spoons
- Mixing bowls
- Saucepans

STEP-BY-STEP PREP

1.   Begin by preparing the **Herbed Quinoa** through step 1 (page 140). While the quinoa cooks, prep the vegetables and herbs, and juice the lemon. When the quinoa is ready, allow it to cool for 5 minutes and then toss with the herb dressing.

2.   Prepare the **Yogurt Parfait with Blueberry Compote** through step 2 (page 28).

3.   While the blueberries are cooking, make the **Lemon-Balsamic Vinaigrette** (page 85).

4.   Stir the blueberry compote. Once it has cooked, set it aside to cool.

5.   Prepare the **Superfood Salad with Lemon-Balsamic Vinaigrette** through step 1 (page 30). While the eggs are cooking, prepare the vegetables and wash the blueberries. Then follow step 2 to properly layer the salad in 2 mason jars.

	BREAKFAST	LUNCH
DAY 1	Yogurt Parfait with Blueberry Compote	Tomato, Asparagus, Basil Flounder with Herbed Quinoa
DAY 2	Yogurt Parfait with Blueberry Compote	Tomato, Asparagus, Basil Flounder with Herbed Quinoa
DAY 3	Yogurt Parfait with Blueberry Compote	Superfood Salad with Lemon-Balsamic Vinaigrette
DAY 4	Yogurt Parfait with Blueberry Compote	Tomato, Asparagus, Basil Flounder with Herbed Quinoa
DAY 5	Yogurt Parfait with Blueberry Compote	Superfood Salad with Lemon-Balsamic Vinaigrette

6. Place the dressing and salads in the refrigerator.

7. Preheat the oven to 425°F.

8. Once the blueberry compote has cooled, finish the yogurt parfaits by layering each of 5 mason jars with ¼ cup of compote, ¾ cup of Greek yogurt, and top with 2 tablespoons of toasted walnuts. Close the jars and place in the refrigerator.

9. Prepare the **Tomato, Asparagus, Basil Flounder** through step 5 (page 29). When baking is complete, line up 4 single-serve reheatable containers. In each, place 1 fish fillet and top with 2 cups of vegetables. Spoon ¾ cup of herbed quinoa on the side of each container. Place 3 containers in the refrigerator for the week, and the fourth can either be frozen or refrigerated for an additional meal.

YOGURT PARFAIT WITH BLUEBERRY COMPOTE

MAKES 5 PARFAITS

PREP TIME: 10 minutes   COOK TIME: 15 minutes

This parfait is a step up from your ho-hum disposable cup of yogurt. The compote is layered at the bottom so you get the "fruit on the bottom" yogurt experience. The crunchy toasted walnuts add texture, as well as an array of nutrients including brain-boosting omega-3 fats, protein, fiber, and numerous B vitamins.

⅔ cup walnuts, chopped

3 cups blueberries, fresh or frozen and thawed

3 tablespoons water

2 tablespoons 100% pure maple syrup

2 teaspoons freshly squeezed lemon juice

1 teaspoon lemon zest

3¾ cups nonfat plain Greek yogurt

1. In a medium saucepan over medium-low heat, toast the walnuts, tossing regularly, until fragrant and lightly browned, about 3 minutes. Remove the toasted walnuts from the saucepan and set aside to cool.

2. In the same saucepan, bring the blueberries, water, maple syrup, and lemon juice and zest to a boil. Reduce the heat to medium-low and simmer, stirring occasionally, until the blueberries have thickened and broken down, about 10 minutes.

3. Remove the saucepan from the heat and set aside for 10 minutes to cool.

4. To assemble the parfaits, layer each of 5 mason glass jars with about ¼ cup of cooled blueberry compote, ¾ cup of yogurt, and 2 tablespoons of walnuts on top.

Refrigerate: Store covered jars in the refrigerator for up to 5 days.

TOBY'S TIP: If you don't have glass jars to layer the parfait, use plastic containers and make a yogurt bowl by placing the ingredients side-by-side. Mix before eating.

Per Parfait: Calories: 266; Total Fat: 11g; Saturated Fat: 1g; Protein: 20g; Total Carbs: 27g; Fiber: 3g; Sugar: 21g; Sodium: 70mg

TOMATO, ASPARAGUS, BASIL FLOUNDER WITH HERBED QUINOA

MAKES 4 SERVINGS

PREP TIME: 15 minutes   COOK TIME: 15 minutes

Roasting is a quick and easy way to cook multiple foods without leaving you with lots of dirty dishes. This sheet pan recipe combines protein-packed, lower-calorie whitefish with colorful vegetables filled with fiber, vitamins, minerals, and antioxidants.

1 bunch asparagus (about 1 pound), woody ends discarded, and cut into thirds

3 tablespoons extra-virgin olive oil, divided

½ teaspoon salt, divided

½ teaspoon freshly ground black pepper, divided

4 (5-ounce) flounder fillets

2 cups cherry tomatoes, halved

¼ cup fresh basil leaves, thinly sliced

Juice and zest of 1 lemon

4 servings (3 cups) Herbed Quinoa (page 140)

1. Preheat the oven to 425°F.

2. In a medium bowl, toss the asparagus with 2 tablespoons of olive oil and ¼ teaspoon each of salt and pepper.

3. Around the outside edges of a baking sheet, spread the asparagus in an even layer, leaving room in the center for the flounder fillets. Lay the fish fillets on the baking sheet, leaving about 1 inch between them.

4. In the same bowl, toss the tomatoes, basil, the remaining 1 tablespoon of olive oil, the remaining ¼ teaspoon of salt and pepper, and the lemon zest and juice. Spoon ½ cup of the tomato mixture evenly over each fish fillet.

5. Bake until the vegetables soften and the fish is flaky and reaches an internal cooking temperature of 145°F, about 15 minutes.

6. Into each of 4 single-serve containers, place 1 fish fillet and top with 2 cups of vegetables. Spoon ¾ cup of Herbed Quinoa on the side.

Storage: Place airtight containers in the refrigerator for up to 4 days. To freeze, place freezer-safe containers in the freezer for up to 2 months. To defrost, refrigerate overnight. To reheat, microwave uncovered on high for 1½ to 2 minutes.

TOBY'S TIP: Any flaky whitefish is perfect for this dish.

Per Serving (1 container): Calories: 492; Total Fat: 26g; Saturated Fat: 4g; Protein: 28g; Total Carbs: 39g; Fiber: 7g; Sugar: 6g; Sodium: 945mg

SUPERFOOD SALAD WITH LEMON-BALSAMIC VINAIGRETTE

MAKES 2 SERVINGS

PREP TIME: 15 minutes   **COOK TIME:** 3 minutes

Salads are so simple to prep, and in them you can include any variety of superfoods that provide vitamins, minerals, and natural plant chemicals your body needs to stay healthy. This one combines antioxidant-filled spinach with blueberries, which contain anthocyanins, powerful anti-inflammatory antioxidants that are beneficial for heart and eye health. The eggs provide protein and the antioxidant lutein, which keeps the heart, eyes, and skin healthy.

2 large eggs

4 tablespoons
  Lemon-Balsamic
  Vinaigrette (page
  85), divided

1 cucumber, cut into ½-inch
  coins, then quartered

1 carrot, peeled and cut
  into ½-inch coins, then
  quartered

¼ small red onion,
  thinly sliced

1 cup fresh blueberries

2½ cups baby spinach

¼ cup roasted unsalted
  sunflower seeds

1.   Hard-boil the eggs by placing them in a medium pot and covering them with water. Over high heat, bring the water to a boil. Cook the eggs for 3 minutes, then remove the pot from the heat, cover, and let stand for 15 minutes. Drain the water and place the eggs in a bowl of ice water until completely cool, about 10 minutes. Peel the eggs and slice lengthwise.

2.   Into each of 2 widemouthed glass mason jars, layer in the following order: 2 tablespoons of Lemon-Balsamic Vinaigrette at the bottom followed by half of the cucumber, carrot, eggs, red onion, blueberries, and baby spinach, and 2 tablespoons of sunflower seeds. If you don't have mason jars, you can use widemouthed glass or plastic containers, in which case add the ingredients in any order that you like but store the dressing separately.

Storage: Place the mason jars or airtight containers in the refrigerator for up to 5 days.

TOBY'S TIP: If using containers instead of mason jars, divide the dressing into 2-tablespoon servings and store on the side.

Per Serving (1 container, plus 2 tablespoons dressing): Calories: 427; Total Fat: 32g; Saturated Fat: 5g; Protein: 13g; Total Carbs: 27g; Fiber: 7g; Sugar: 14g; Sodium: 305mg

MEAL PREP 3

THIS PREP WEEK OFFERS a repertoire of proteins including tofu, turkey, and chicken, allowing you to have a meatless meal four days of the week. The Rise and Shine Breakfast Cookies are a healthy "indulgence" for 150 calories each. If you want to up your calories for the meal, pair the cookie with a cup of Greek yogurt or glass of milk. You'll also have two extra Lighter Chicken Potpies, which you can freeze for a later date or save for the weekend (they're so good, I'm not sure you'll want to share!).

≪ Turkey Meatballs with Carrots over Zucchini Noodles (page 40)

MEAL PREP 3

SHOPPING LIST

PANTRY

- Applesauce, unsweetened (½ cup)
- Baking soda
- Black pepper, freshly ground
- Broth, low-sodium chicken (1½ cups)
- Broth, low-sodium vegetable (2 cups)
- Brown sugar
- Canola oil
- Chiles, red or green diced (1 [4-ounce] can)
- Cinnamon, ground
- Dijon mustard
- Flour, all-purpose, unbleached
- Flour, whole-wheat pastry
- Honey
- Maple syrup, 100% pure
- Nonstick cooking spray
- Nutmeg, ground
- Oats, rolled
- Olive oil
- Olive oil, extra virgin
- Panko bread crumbs, whole-wheat
- Quinoa
- Red pepper flakes
- Rice vinegar
- Salt
- Sesame oil, toasted
- Tomatoes, whole peeled plum (1 [28-ounce] can)
- Vanilla extract

FRUIT, VEGETABLES & HERBS

- Basil, fresh (1 bunch)
- Broccoli (1 crown, about 1 pound)
- Carrots (1 pound bag)
- Celery (1 bunch)
- Garlic (2 heads)
- Lemons (2)
- Mushrooms, white (4 ounces)
- Onions, small (2)
- Parsley (2 bunches)
- Raisins, golden (¾ cup)

- Scallions (1 bunch)
- Shallot (1)
- Thyme (1 bunch)
- Zucchini (3 medium)

PROTEIN

- Eggs, large (3)
- Rotisserie chicken (1)
- Tofu, extra-firm (1 [12-ounce] package)
- Turkey, 90% to 94% lean ground (1 pound)

DAIRY

- Milk, reduced-fat (2%) (1 quart)

FROZEN

- Peas (1 [10-ounce] package)
- Phyllo dough sheets (1 package)

EQUIPMENT

- Baking sheets
- Chef's knife
- Cutting board
- Grill pan
- Measuring cups and spoons
- Mixing bowls
- Parchment paper
- Ramekins or individual ovenproof dishes
- Skillet

STEP-BY-STEP PREP

1. Preheat the oven to 350°F.

2. Prepare the **Rise and Shine Breakfast Cookies** through step 5 (page 36), and place in the oven to bake.

3. Prepare the **Chile-Garlic Sauce** (page 88). Remove the cookies from

	BREAKFAST	LUNCH	DINNER
DAY 1	Rise and Shine Breakfast Cookies	Asian-Style Tofu Bowl	Turkey Meatballs with Carrots over Zucchini Noodles
DAY 2	Rise and Shine Breakfast Cookies	Asian-Style Tofu Bowl	Turkey Meatballs with Carrots over Zucchini Noodles
DAY 3	Rise and Shine Breakfast Cookies	Turkey Meatballs with Carrots over Zucchini Noodles	Lighter Chicken Potpie
DAY 4	Rise and Shine Breakfast Cookies	Asian-Style Tofu Bowl	Turkey Meatballs with Carrots over Zucchini Noodles
DAY 5	Rise and Shine Breakfast Cookies	Asian-Style Tofu Bowl	Lighter Chicken Potpie

the oven and set aside to cool. Raise the oven temperature to 450°F.

4. Prepare the tofu for the **Asian-Style Tofu Bowl** through step 1 (page 38).

5. Prepare the **Roasted Broccoli with Shallots** through step 4 (page 148), and place in the oven to roast.

6. Prepare the **Chunky Tomato Sauce** through step 1 (page 89). Remove the broccoli from the oven and set aside to cool.

7. Prepare the **Zucchini Noodles with Lemon Vinaigrette** through step 2 (page 146). Set the noodles aside.

8. Remove the tomato sauce from the stove and set aside to cool.

9. Prepare the **Herbed Quinoa** through step 1 (page 140). While the quinoa cooks, grill the tofu from the **Asian-Style Tofu Bowl** through step 2 (page 38). Finish through step 2 of the quinoa and set aside. Complete step 3 of the tofu bowls.

10. Prepare the **Turkey Meatballs with Carrots over Zucchini Noodles** through step 2 (page 40). While the meatballs cook, measure and prep the vegetables for the **Lighter Chicken Potpie** (page 39). When the meatballs are cooked, finish through step 5 of the turkey meatballs recipe.

11. Preheat the oven to 400°F.

12. Prepare the **Lighter Chicken Potpie** through step 5 (page 39).

RISE AND SHINE BREAKFAST COOKIES

MAKES 20 COOKIES

PREP TIME: 15 minutes   COOK TIME: 15 minutes

You *can* have cookies for breakfast! Enjoy this delicious grab-and-go breakfast with a glass of low-fat milk or your morning cup of joe. They're made with whole-grain oats, whole-wheat pastry flour, applesauce, raisins, and yes—carrots. The carrots not only provide sweetness but are also a source of the antioxidant vitamin A, which helps maintain good eyesight and helps protect the body from certain types of cancer and heart disease.

Nonstick cooking spray

½ cup rolled oats

1¼ cups unbleached all-purpose flour

1 cup whole-wheat pastry flour

1 teaspoon ground cinnamon

1 teaspoon baking soda

¼ teaspoon ground nutmeg

¼ teaspoon salt

½ cup unsweetened applesauce

½ cup packed brown sugar

½ cup 100% pure maple syrup

¼ cup canola oil

2 large eggs, beaten

1 teaspoon vanilla extract

2 large carrots, shredded

¾ cup golden raisins

1. Preheat the oven to 350°F. Line two baking sheets with parchment paper and coat with cooking spray.

2. In a medium bowl, mix togther the oats, all-purpose and whole-wheat flours, cinnamon, baking soda, nutmeg, and salt.

3. In a large bowl, whisk together the applesauce, brown sugar, maple syrup, oil, eggs, and vanilla until smooth and creamy.

4. Gently fold the dry ingredients into the wet ingredients, and stir until just combined. Fold in the carrots and raisins to evenly distribute throughout the batter.

5. For each cookie, drop 2 tablespoons of batter onto the prepared baking sheets, leaving about 2 inches between each cookie. Using clean hands, gently press down on the top of each cookie to slightly flatten them.

6. Bake for about 15 minutes until the cookies are soft and golden brown and a toothpick inserted into the center of 1 or 2 cookies comes out clean. Let cool for 5 minutes.

Storage: Store the cookies in an airtight container at room temperature for up to 5 days. To freeze, individually wrap each cookie in plastic wrap and freeze for up to 2 months. To defrost, leave on the countertop overnight. To reheat, warm in the toaster oven at 350°F for about 10 minutes or microwave uncovered on high for 30 to 45 seconds.

TOBY'S TIP: If the cookie batter sticks to your hands, wet your hands with lukewarm water before handling it.

Per Serving (1 cookie): Calories: 150; Total Fat: 4g; Saturated Fat: 0g; Protein: 2g; Total Carbs: 28g; Fiber: 2g; Sugar: 15g; Sodium: 86mg

ASIAN-STYLE TOFU BOWL

MAKES 4 SERVINGS

PREP TIME: 15 minutes   **COOK TIME:** 5 minutes

Tofu is a high-quality protein that provides all the essential amino acids your body needs, making it a complete protein—rare for a plant-derived food. If you've never had tofu, here's a little insight: It's really versatile. It absorbs the flavor of whatever it's mixed with and can be used in anything from smoothies to chocolate pudding to savory dishes like stir-fries and this bowl.

1 (12-ounce) package extra-firm tofu, drained and cut into 8 slices

2 servings (5 tablespoons) Chile-Garlic Sauce (page 88)

Nonstick cooking spray

4 servings (3 cups) Herbed Quinoa (page 140)

4 servings (4 cups) Roasted Broccoli with Shallots (page 148)

1.   Place the tofu in a medium bowl. Add the Chile-Garlic Sauce. Cover and refrigerate for at least 30 minutes and up to 2 hours.

2.   Heat a grill pan on high and coat with cooking spray. Grill the tofu until golden, 2 minutes on each side. Remove the tofu from the grill pan and set aside to cool.

3.   Into each of 4 containers, spoon ¾ cup of Herbed Quinoa, 1 cup of Roasted Broccoli with Shallots, and 2 pieces of grilled tofu.

Storage: Place airtight containers in the refrigerator for up to 1 week. To freeze, place freezer-safe containers in the freezer for up to 2 months. To defrost, refrigerate overnight. To reheat, microwave uncovered on high for 1 to 2 minutes.

TOBY'S TIP: Mix things up by marinating this tofu in the Meal Prep Barbecue Sauce (page 90).

Per Serving (1 container): Calories: 521; Total Fat: 33g; Saturated Fat: 4g; Protein: 18g; Total Carbs: 42g; Fiber: 4g; Sugar: 4g; Sodium: 511mg

LIGHTER CHICKEN POTPIE

MAKES 4 SERVINGS

PREP TIME: 20 minutes   COOK TIME: 25 minutes

Filled with vegetables and chicken, this all-in-one dish gets its lower-calorie crunch by using frozen phyllo dough. You can find phyllo dough sheets in the frozen section of your grocery store, by the pie shells.

3 tablespoons canola oil or safflower oil, divided

1 small onion, chopped

1 garlic clove, minced

2 celery stalks, chopped

3 medium carrots, chopped

4 ounces white mushrooms, thinly sliced (8 mushrooms)

2 tablespoons unbleached all-purpose flour

1½ cups low-sodium chicken or vegetable broth

1½ cups reduced-fat (2%) milk

1½ cups shredded cooked skinless, boneless chicken or rotisserie chicken

1 cup frozen peas

2 tablespoons chopped fresh parsley

1 tablespoon fresh thyme

¼ teaspoon salt

¼ teaspoon freshly ground black pepper

4 sheets frozen phyllo dough, thawed

1. Preheat the oven to 400°F.

2. In a large skillet over medium heat, heat 2 tablespoons of oil. Add the onion, garlic, celery, carrots, and mushrooms, and sauté until the vegetables soften, about 5 minutes. Sprinkle the vegetable mixture with the flour and cook for 2 minutes. Add the broth, milk, chicken, and peas, and bring to a boil. Reduce the heat and simmer, stirring occasionally, until the mixture is thick and creamy, about 8 minutes. Stir in the parsley, thyme, salt, and pepper.

3. Evenly divide the chicken filling among 4 ramekins or individual oven-safe dishes.

4. Carefully divide each phyllo sheet in two. Place 2 pieces of phyllo dough over the top of each dish. Brush the phyllo dough sheets with the remaining 1 tablespoon of oil.

5. Place the individual dishes on a baking sheet. Bake until the phyllo dough is golden brown, about 10 minutes. Remove from the oven and set aside to cool for 10 to 15 minutes.

Storage: Cover with plastic wrap and store in the refrigerator for up to 1 week. To freeze, cover the pies with aluminum foil or plastic wrap and freeze for up to 1 month. To defrost, refrigerate overnight. To reheat, microwave uncovered for 2 to 3 minutes.

TOBY'S TIP: Starting to accumulate leftover frozen veggies? Frozen carrots, broccoli, string beans, or any combo are perfect add-ins for a chicken potpie. Add them into the creamy sauce when you add the peas.

Per Serving (1 individual pie): Calories: 384; Total Fat: 16g; Saturated Fat: 3g; Protein: 26g; Total Carbs: 35g; Fiber: 5g; Sugar: 11g; Sodium: 633mg

TURKEY MEATBALLS WITH CARROTS OVER ZUCCHINI NOODLES

MAKES 4 SERVINGS

PREP TIME: 25 minutes   **COOK TIME:** 20 minutes

Zucchini, carrot, or another spiralized vegetable makes a terrific low-calorie and low-carb substitute for grain pasta. However, you can always opt for whole-wheat spaghetti or any type of alternative pasta like quinoa, bean, legume, or rice. Just follow the directions on the manufacturer's label for appropriate cooking times.

1 pound ground turkey (90% to 94% lean)

2 medium carrots, shredded

1 small onion, finely chopped

1 garlic clove, minced

1 large egg, beaten

½ cup whole-wheat panko bread crumbs

½ cup finely chopped fresh parsley

¼ teaspoon salt

¼ teaspoon freshly ground black pepper

2 tablespoons olive oil

4 servings (6 cups) Zucchini Noodles with Lemon Vinaigrette (page 146)

4 servings (2 cups) Chunky Tomato Sauce (page 89)

1. In a large bowl, mix together the turkey, carrots, onion, garlic, egg, bread crumbs, parsley, salt, and pepper.

2. Shape 1 heaping teaspoon of turkey mixture into a ball, and place it on a large plate. Repeat with the remaining mixture to make about 20 meatballs.

3. In a large skillet over medium heat, heat the oil until shimmering. Add the meatballs and cook, covered, turning the meatballs occasionally until browned on all sides and a thermometer inserted into a meatball reads 165°F, 15 to 18 minutes.

4. Using a slotted spoon, transfer the meatballs to a clean plate.

5. Into each of 4 containers, place 1½ cups of Zucchini Noodles with Lemon Vinaigrette and top with 5 meatballs and ½ cup of Chunky Tomato Sauce.

Storage: Place airtight containers in the refrigerator for up to 5 days. To freeze, place the turkey meatballs and tomato sauce (without the Zucchini Noodles with Lemon Vinaigrette) in freezer-safe containers in the freezer for up to 2 months. To defrost, refrigerate overnight. To reheat, microwave uncovered on high for 2 to 3 minutes. Alternatively, reheat the entire batch of meatballs and sauce in a medium saucepan on the stove top. Bring to a boil, reduce the heat, and simmer until heated through, 10 to 15 minutes.

TOBY'S TIP: Opt for ground turkey that's 90% to 94% lean. The little bit of fat will help keep the meatballs moist.

Per Serving (1 container): Calories: 458; Total Fat: 28g; Saturated Fat: 5g; Protein: 29g; Total Carbs: 27g; Fiber: 6g; Sugar: 13g; Sodium: 992mg

MEAL PREP 4

YOU'LL FIND LOTS OF CHEESY goodness in this week's meal selection. Don't worry—I kept the calories, saturated fat, and sodium under control without compromising any flavor! From a spin on chicken Parmesan to a lightened-up version of lasagna, this week's meals and snack are filling, delicious, nutritious, and easy to make. This week we'll also explore some simple healthy cooking hacks to lighten dishes. For example, in my Beef Lasagna (page 52), I use a blend of portobello mushrooms and lean ground beef. These are tricks I've been using for years to lighten up my dishes, and hopefully now you can use them to lighten your favorites, too.

≪ Lighter Waldorf Salad with Pears (page 49)

SHOPPING LIST

PANTRY

- Anchovy paste
- Balsamic vinegar
- Basil, dried
- Black pepper, freshly ground
- Broth, low-sodium vegetable (1 [32-ounce] container)
- Chickpeas, low-sodium (1 [15-ounce] can)
- Dijon mustard
- Honey
- Lasagna noodles, whole-wheat oven-ready (1 [8-ounce] box)
- Mayonnaise, reduced-fat
- Nonstick cooking spray
- Olive oil
- Olive oil, extra virgin
- Oregano, dried
- Pita, 4-inch whole-wheat (1 [5-pita] package)
- Quinoa
- Salt
- Sriracha
- Tahini (sesame seed paste)
- Tomatoes, no-sodium-added, diced (1 [14.5-ounce] can)
- Tomato paste
- Tomato sauce, (1 [15-ounce] can)
- Walnuts

FRUIT, VEGETABLES, HERBS & SPICES

- Avocado (1)
- Basil, fresh (2 bunches)
- Carrots (1 [1-pound] bag)
- Celery (1 [1-pound] package)
- Cucumbers, Kirby or Persian (3)
- Garlic (1 head)
- Grapes, seedless red (1 small bunch)
- Lemons (6)
- Lettuce, Bibb or other green lettuce (1 small head)
- Mushrooms, portobello caps (8 ounces)
- Onion, yellow (1)
- Parsley, fresh (2 bunches)
- Pear (1)
- Scallions (2)
- Tomatoes, plum (5)

PROTEIN

- Beef, ground, 90% lean (1 pound)
- Chicken breast, skinless, boneless (8 ounces)
- Chicken breast cutlets, skinless, boneless (1¼ pounds)
- Eggs, large (6)

DAIRY

- Greek yogurt, nonfat plain, (1 [32-ounce] container)
- Mozzarella cheese ball, fresh, part-skim (8 ounces)
- Mozzarella cheese, shredded, part-skim (8 ounces)
- Parmesan cheese, grated (1 cup)
- Ricotta cheese, part-skim (1 [15-ounce] container)
- Swiss cheese (5 slices)

EQUIPMENT

- 11-by-14-inch baking dish
- Baking sheet
- Chef's knife
- Cutting board
- Grill pan
- Measuring cups and spoons
- Mixing bowls
- Saucepans
- Skillet

	BREAKFAST	LUNCH	DINNER	SNACK
DAY 1	Israeli Breakfast with Pita	Lighter Waldorf Salad with Pears	Balsamic Chicken Breast with Mozzarella and Tomato	Green Goddess Vegetable Jars
DAY 2	Israeli Breakfast with Pita	Lighter Waldorf Salad with Pears	Beef Lasagna	Green Goddess Vegetable Jars
DAY 3	Israeli Breakfast with Pita	Beef Lasagna	Balsamic Chicken Breast with Mozzarella and Tomato	Green Goddess Vegetable Jars
DAY 4	Israeli Breakfast with Pita	Balsamic Chicken Breast with Mozzarella and Tomato	Beef Lasagna	Green Goddess Vegetable Jars
DAY 5	Israeli Breakfast with Pita	Balsamic Chicken Breast with Mozzarella and Tomato	Beef Lasagna	Green Goddess Vegetable Jars

STEP-BY-STEP PREP

1.   Prepare the **Beef Lasagna** through step 1 (page 52).

2.   While the ground beef is cooking, prepare the hummus for **Simple Hummus with Vegetables** through step 1 (page 152).

3.   Prepare the **Israeli Breakfast with Pita** through step 1 (page 47). While the eggs are cooking and

cooling, prep the bowls, leaving space for the egg.

4.   Prepare the **Green Goddess Dressing** (page 84).

5.   Remove the ground beef from the stove and set aside to cool. Preheat the oven to 350˚F. Continue making the **Beef Lasagna**, steps 3 through 6 (page 52).

6.   Prepare and assemble the **Green Goddess Vegetable Jars** (page 48).

CONTINUED ▶

7. Cook the quinoa for the **Herbed Quinoa** in step 1 (page 140). While the quinoa is cooking, make the **Lemon-Balsamic Vinaigrette** (page 85), and marinate the chicken breasts for the **Balsamic Chicken Breast with Mozzarella and Tomato**, step 1 (page 50).

8. Finish preparing the **Herbed Quinoa**. Remove the lasagna from the oven, raise the oven temperature to 375'F, and allow the lasagna to cool before packing into 8 containers. Place 4 in the refrigerator, and the extra 4 in the freezer.

9. Prepare the **Lighter Waldorf Salad with Pears** through step 6 (page 49).

10. Remove the marinated chicken from the refrigerator, and prepare the **Balsamic Chicken Breast with Mozzarella and Tomato**, steps 2 through 5 (page 50).

ISRAELI BREAKFAST WITH PITA

MAKES 5 SERVINGS

PREP TIME: 15 minutes   **COOK TIME:** 5 minutes

Start your day with this savory breakfast that's got it all—protein, vegetables, whole grains, dairy, and healthy fat. The combo of fiber, protein, and healthy fat will help keep you satisfied so you can power through any busy morning.

5 large eggs

5 slices low-fat Swiss cheese

5 servings (1¼ cups) hummus only from Simple Hummus with Vegetables (page 152)

3 plum tomatoes, sliced

3 Kirby or Persian cucumbers

5 (4-inch) whole-wheat pitas, halved

1.   Hard-boil the eggs by placing them in a medium pot and covering them with water. Over high heat, bring the water to a boil. Cook the eggs for 3 minutes, then remove the pot from the heat, cover, and let stand for 15 minutes. Drain the water, and place the eggs in a bowl of ice water until completely cool, about 10 minutes. Peel the eggs and slice lengthwise.

2.   Into each of 5 resealable containers, place a folded slice of Swiss cheese. Top each with a sliced egg. Spoon the hummus on the side, and set the tomatoes and cucumbers next to the hummus. Place 2 pita halves in each container.

Storage: Place airtight containers in the refrigerator for up to 5 days.

TOBY'S TIP: To avoid the pita getting soggy, wrap in plastic wrap before sealing the container or store separately until ready to eat.

Per Serving (1 container): Calories: 408; Total Fat: 21g; Saturated Fat: 4g; Protein: 21g; Total Carbs: 38g; Fiber: 8g; Sugar: 6g; Sodium: 878mg

GREEN GODDESS VEGETABLE JARS

MAKES 5 JARS

PREP TIME: 15 minutes

Vegetables are so much tastier when you can dip them in something delicious. Even better is when the dressing is nutritious! The Green Goddess Dressing is made with avocado and Greek yogurt, which together provide healthy fat and protein. Pair this dressing with fiber-filled vegetables and you've got a snack that's a winner in both categories: healthy *and* delicious.

5 servings (10 tablespoons) Green Goddess Dressing (page 84), divided

10 medium carrots, peeled, trimmed, sliced lengthwise, then halved

10 celery stalks, washed, trimmed, and halved

1. Into each of 5 mason jars, spoon 2 tablespoons of Green Goddess Dressing.

2. Stand the vegetable sticks upright in the dressing.

Storage: Place airtight jars in the refrigerator for up to 5 days.

TOBY'S TIP: Swap the vegetables to your liking—you can also use leftover veggies like bell peppers, jicama, and zucchini.

Per Serving (1 jar): Calories: 124; Total Fat: 6g; Saturated Fat: 1g; Protein: 3g; Total Carbs: 18g; Fiber: 7g; Sugar: 8g; Sodium: 248mg

LIGHTER WALDORF SALAD WITH PEARS

MAKES 2 SERVINGS

PREP TIME: 15 minutes   COOK TIME: 15 minutes

Traditional Waldorf salads can rack up hundreds of calories from the mayonnaise-based dressing alone, but that payload is just not necessary! This lighter version swaps part of the mayonnaise for nonfat plain Greek yogurt, which helps maintain creaminess and delicious flavor.

¼ cup walnuts, roughly chopped

8 ounces skinless, boneless chicken breast

¼ teaspoon salt, divided

¼ teaspoon freshly ground black pepper, divided

1 tablespoon olive oil

¼ cup reduced-fat mayonnaise

3 tablespoons nonfat plain Greek yogurt

2 teaspoons freshly squeezed lemon juice

1 teaspoon honey

Small head Bibb or other green lettuce, roughly chopped (about 3½ cups)

1 medium pear, halved, cored, and thinly sliced

½ cup seedless red grapes, halved

1 celery stalk, diced

1.   In a small skillet over medium-low heat, toast the walnuts, stirring occasionally, until slightly browned, 3 to 4 minutes. Remove from the heat and set aside to cool.

2.   Sprinkle both sides of the chicken breast with ⅛ teaspoon of salt and pepper.

3.   In a grill pan or skillet over medium heat, heat the oil. Add the chicken breast and cook for about 10 minutes, turning once, until it reaches a minimum internal cooking temperature of 165°F. Allow to cool for 10 minutes and then dice.

4.   In a large bowl, whisk together the mayonnaise, yogurt, lemon juice, honey, and remaining ⅛ teaspoon of salt and ⅛ teaspoon of pepper.

5.   Add the walnuts, chicken, lettuce, pear, grapes, and celery, tossing to evenly coat.

6.   Divide the salad between 2 resealable containers, about 3 cups per container.

Storage: Place airtight containers in the refrigerator up to 5 days.

> **TOBY'S TIP:** Swap the pear for an apple for a traditional spin on this salad.

Per Serving (1 container): Calories: 397; Total Fat: 19g; Saturated Fat: 3g; Protein: 30g; Total Carbs: 28g; Fiber: 5g; Sugar: 19g; Sodium: 624mg

BALSAMIC CHICKEN BREAST WITH MOZZARELLA AND TOMATO

MAKES 4 SERVINGS

PREP TIME: 15 minutes, plus 30 minutes marinating time   **COOK TIME:** 20 minutes

Mozzarella cheese imparts wonderful flavor, but it also provides essential nutrients like protein, calcium, vitamin B_{12}, riboflavin, phosphorus, zinc, and selenium. Plus, mozzarella is a lactose-intolerant-friendly food, which makes it easier for those with lactose intolerance to digest. *Buon appetito!*

4 thin skinless, boneless
  chicken cutlets
  (1¼ pounds)

2 servings (¼ cup)
  Lemon-Balsamic
  Vinaigrette (page 85)

Nonstick cooking spray

8 ounces fresh mozzarella,
  cut into 4 slices

2 plum tomatoes, thinly cut
  into 8 round slices

1 tablespoon
  balsamic vinegar

¼ cup fresh basil, cut
  into ribbons

4 servings (3 cups) Herbed
  Quinoa (page 140)

1.   Place the chicken breasts in a medium bowl and toss with the Lemon-Balsamic Vinaigrette. Cover and refrigerate for at least 30 minutes and up to overnight.

2.   Preheat the oven to 375°F.

3.   Coat a large skillet with cooking spray and heat over medium heat. When the oil is shimmering, add the chicken cutlets. Discard the excess marinade. Cook for about 10 minutes, flipping once, until the chicken is browned and has reached an internal cooking temperature of at least 165°F.

4.   Top each chicken breast with 1 slice of cheese and 2 slices of tomato. Cover the skillet and cook until the cheese is slightly melted, 10 minutes more. Drizzle the chicken with the balsamic vinegar and sprinkle with the basil.

5.   Into each of 4 resealable containers, place ¾ cup of Herbed Quinoa and top with 1 chicken breast.

Storage: Place airtight containers in the refrigerator for up to 1 week. To reheat, microwave uncovered on high for about 2 minutes.

> **TOBY'S TIP:** I prefer fresh mozzarella when available, but you can also find presliced mozzarella in the dairy aisle or deli counter.

Per Serving (1 container): Calories: 516; Total Fat: 31g; Saturated Fat: 9g; Protein: 24g; Total Carbs: 35g; Fiber: 4g; Sugar: 4g; Sodium: 660mg

BEEF LASAGNA

MAKES 8 SERVINGS

PREP TIME: 20 minutes   **COOK TIME:** 1 hour 30 minutes

To lighten up the dish and for an extra boost of flavor, I like to use an even combination of lean ground beef and portobello mushrooms. This "blending" technique can be used for other ground-beef dishes such as meatloaf, burgers, chili, and meat sauce.

1 tablespoon olive oil

2 garlic cloves, minced

1 medium onion, chopped

8 ounces portobello mushrooms, chopped

1 pound 90% lean ground beef

1 (14.5-ounce) can no-salt-added diced tomatoes

2 tablespoons tomato paste

1 tablespoon dried oregano

2 teaspoons dried basil

2 teaspoons Sriracha

1 cup grated Parmesan cheese, divided

1¼ cups part-skim ricotta cheese

1 (8-ounce) package part-skim mozzarella cheese, divided

1 large egg, beaten

¼ cup chopped fresh parsley

1 (15-ounce) can tomato sauce or 1¾ cups Chunky Tomato Sauce (page 89)

9 whole-wheat oven-ready lasagna noodles

1. In a large saucepan over medium heat, heat the oil. When shimmering, add the garlic and onion and cook, stirring frequently, until the onion is translucent and the garlic is fragrant, about 4 minutes. Add the mushrooms and cook until they begin to soften, about 5 minutes. Add the ground beef and cook, breaking up with a wooden spoon, until browned, about 5 minutes. Add the diced tomatoes, tomato paste, oregano, basil, and Sriracha, and bring to a boil. Reduce the heat and simmer, covered, for about 35 minutes.

2. Meanwhile, preheat the oven to 350°F.

3. In a medium bowl, combine ¾ cup of Parmesan, the ricotta, ¾ cup of mozzarella, the egg, and parsley. Mix to blend.

4. Spoon ¼ cup of tomato sauce on the bottom of an 11-by-14-inch baking dish, spreading evenly with the back of the spoon.

5. Fill a large flat container with water. Dip each of 3 lasagna noodles in the water, shake off the excess water, and place on the bottom of the baking dish side by side, overlapping them as little as possible. Top with half the cheese mixture and half of the meat sauce. Repeat the layer with the lasagna noodles dipped in water, following by the remaining half of the cheese mixture, and remaining half of the meat sauce. Top with the last 3 noodles, dipped in water, and spread the remaining 1½ cups of tomato sauce over the top. Sprinkle the top with the remaining ¼ cup of grated Parmesan and remaining mozzarella.

6.   Cover the lasagna with aluminum foil and bake for 40 minutes until the cheese has melted and the top is slightly browned. Uncover and bake for an additional 10 minutes. Remove from the oven and allow to cool for at least 10 minutes before slicing into 8 pieces.

7.   Into each of 8 resealable containers, place 1 piece of lasagna.

Storage: Place airtight containers in the refrigerator for up to 1 week. To freeze, place freezer-safe containers in the freezer for up to 2 months. To defrost, refrigerate overnight. To reheat, microwave uncovered on high for 2 to 3 minutes. Alternatively, reheat several pieces of thawed lasagna in a 350°F oven until warmed through, 10 to 15 minutes.

> **TOBY'S TIP:** Although olive oil is a healthy fat, it is important to measure out oil portions carefully. As all oils contain 120 calories per tablespoon, it's easy to overpour and rack up unnecessary calories.

Per Serving (1 piece): Calories: 466; Total Fat: 22g; Saturated Fat: 11g; Protein: 35g; Total Carbs: 32g; Fiber: 6g; Sugar: 8g; Sodium: 844mg

MEAL PREP 5

THIS WEEK IT'S ALL ABOUT healthy ways to enjoy comfort foods. You can enjoy a balanced, varied, and healthy diet with all your favorite foods. You'll find eggs for breakfast, pasta salad for lunch, meatloaf for dinner, and even a healthy chocolate pudding as a snack. Each meal is balanced with a protein, starch or whole grain, and vegetable; the snack is made with dairy and fruit. If you choose to have one or two more snacks per day, depending on the number of calories you need and your activity level, make sure these snacks include fruits and/or vegetables.

≪ Rosemary–Honey Mustard Pork Tenderloin with Lemon-Dill Carrots (page 64)

SHOPPING LIST

PANTRY

- Apple cider vinegar
- Balsamic vinegar
- Bay leaves, dried
- Black pepper, freshly ground
- Broth, low-sodium vegetable (1 [14.5-ounce] can)
- Brown sugar
- Cocoa powder, unsweetened
- Cornstarch
- Dijon mustard
- Honey
- Ketchup
- Lentils, low-sodium brown (2 [15-ounce] cans)
- Maple syrup, 100% pure
- Nonstick cooking spray
- Oats, quick cooking
- Oil, coconut
- Olive oil
- Paprika, smoked
- Pasta, whole-wheat farfalle (8 ounces)
- Rice, long-grain brown
- Salt
- Vanilla extract
- White wine vinegar
- Worcestershire sauce

FRUIT, VEGETABLES, HERBS & SPICES

- Carrots, baby (1 pound)
- Carrots (2)
- Dill (1 bunch)
- Garlic (1 head)
- Lemon (1)
- Onions, yellow (2)
- Potatoes, sweet (4)
- Raspberries, fresh (1 [6-ounce] container)
- Rosemary (1 bunch)
- Shallot (1)
- Spinach, fresh (1 [10-ounce] bag)
- Tomatoes, cherry (1 pound)
- Zucchini (1 medium)

PROTEIN

- Beef, 90% lean ground (1 pound)
- Eggs, large (11)
- Pork tenderloin, boneless (1¼ pounds)

DAIRY

- Milk, 2% reduced-fat (1 quart)
- Mozzarella, fresh, cherry-size balls (6 ounces)
- Parmesan, shredded (⅓ cup)

FROZEN

- Edamame, shelled (1 [10-ounce] package)

EQUIPMENT

- 9-by-5-inch loaf pan
- Baking sheet
- Chef's knife
- Cutting board
- Measuring cups and spoons
- Mixing bowls
- Saucepans
- Skillet

	BREAKFAST	LUNCH	DINNER	SNACK
DAY 1	Mini Spinach Frittatas	Caprese Whole-Grain Pasta Salad with Edamame	Veggie-Lovers' Meatloaf with Baked Sweet Potato	Chocolate Pudding with Raspberries
DAY 2	Mini Spinach Frittatas	Rosemary–Honey Mustard Pork Tenderloin with Lemon-Dill Carrots	Veggie-Lovers' Meatloaf with Baked Sweet Potato	Chocolate Pudding with Raspberries
DAY 3	Mini Spinach Frittatas	Caprese Whole-Grain Pasta Salad with Edamame	Rosemary–Honey Mustard Pork Tenderloin with Lemon-Dill Carrots	Chocolate Pudding with Raspberries
DAY 4	Mini Spinach Frittatas	Caprese Whole-Grain Pasta Salad with Edamame	Veggie-Lovers' Meatloaf with Baked Sweet Potato	Chocolate Pudding with Raspberries
DAY 5	Mini Spinach Frittatas	Caprese Whole-Grain Pasta Salad with Edamame	Veggie-Lovers' Meatloaf with Baked Sweet Potato	Chocolate Pudding with Raspberries

STEP-BY-STEP PREP

1. Prepare the **Veggie-Lovers' Meatloaf with Baked Sweet Potato** through step 2 (page 62).

2. Prepare the **Meal Prep Barbecue Sauce** (page 90).

3. While the sweet potatoes are cooking, prepare the meatloaf for the **Veggie-Lovers' Meatloaf with Baked Sweet Potato**, steps 3 through 5 (page 62). Set the uncooked meatloaf aside.

4. Fully prepare the **Caprese Whole-Grain Pasta Salad with Edamame** (page 59).

5. Fully prepare the **Lemon-Dill Carrots** (page 149). Set aside.

6. When done, remove the sweet potatoes from the oven and reduce the oven temperature to 350°F. Bake the meatloaf for 1 hour, step 6 (page 62).

CONTINUED ▶

7.　While the meatloaf is cooking, create the marinade for the **Rosemary–Honey Mustard Pork Tenderloin** and marinate the pork, step 1 (page 64).

8.　Prepare the **Mini Spinach Frittatas**, steps 1 through 4 (page 60). Set the uncooked frittatas aside.

9.　Fully prepare the **Chocolate Pudding with Raspberries** (page 65).

10.　When the meatloaf is cooked, set it aside to cool, step 7 (page 63). Bake the **Mini Spinach Frittatas** for 30 minutes, step 5 (page 60).

11.　Meanwhile, cook the rice for the **Brown Rice with Lentils**, step 1 (page 142).

12.　Once the **Mini Spinach Frittatas** (page 60) are cooked, set aside to cool. Increase the oven temperature to 400˚F. Once the oven is preheated, remove the pork tenderloin from the refrigerator and place on a baking sheet to cook for 40 minutes.

13.　While the pork tenderloin is cooking, finish preparing the **Brown Rice with Lentils** (page 142).

14.　Complete the **Veggie-Lovers' Meatloaf** (page 62).

15.　Once the pork is cooked, complete the **Rosemary–Honey Mustard Pork Tenderloin with Lemon-Dill Carrots** (page 64).

CAPRESE WHOLE-GRAIN PASTA SALAD WITH EDAMAME

MAKES 4 SERVINGS

PREP TIME: 10 minutes   COOK TIME: 10 minutes

Whole grains are an important part of a healthy eating plan. Whether you're trying to lose weight or just maintain it, make sure that half your daily grain is whole grain. Benefits of whole grains include maintaining gut health, decreasing the risk of colon cancer, reducing blood cholesterol, and helping keep you satisfied. Examples of whole grains include whole-wheat pasta, quinoa, brown rice, 100 percent whole-wheat bread, sorghum, millet, and oats. If some sound foreign to you, give them a whirl!

8 ounces whole-wheat farfalle pasta

1 cup frozen shelled edamame

¼ cup balsamic vinegar

2 tablespoons olive oil

¼ teaspoon salt

1 cup cherry tomatoes (about 20), halved

1 (6-ounce) container "cherry size" mozzarella balls, halved

1. Fill a medium saucepan ¾ of the way full with water and bring to a boil. Add the pasta, gently stir, and return to a boil. Continue cooking, uncovered and stirring occasionally, for 6 minutes. Gently add the edamame to the pasta and return to a boil. Continue cooking, stirring occasionally, about 5 minutes or until the pasta is al dente and the edamame is heated through. Set aside to cool for 10 minutes.

2. In a medium bowl, whisk together the balsamic vinegar, oil, and salt until thoroughly blended. Add the cooled pasta and edamame, gently folding to evenly coat.

3. Add the tomatoes and mozzarella, and gently fold to combine.

4. Into each of 4 containers, place one-quarter of the pasta salad.

Storage: Place airtight containers in the refrigerator for up to 5 days. Enjoy cold.

TOBY'S TIP: Edamame, or baby soybeans, are added for protein. You can replace them with cooked chicken or turkey instead.

Per Serving (1 container): Calories: 456; Total Fat: 19g; Saturated Fat: 6g; Protein: 25g; Total Carbs: 47g; Fiber: 6g; Sugar: 7g; Sodium: 456mg

MINI SPINACH FRITTATAS

MAKES 10 FRITTATAS

PREP TIME: 20 minutes   COOK TIME: 30 minutes

According to the Dietary Guidelines for Americans, 90 percent of Americans don't meet their recommended daily vegetable needs. Adding vegetables to your morning can help close the gap and ensure you're racking up those vital nutrients for the day.

Nonstick cooking spray

1 teaspoon olive oil

1 garlic clove, minced

3 cups fresh spinach, washed and trimmed

10 large eggs

¼ cup water

¼ teaspoon salt

1 cup cherry tomatoes (about 20), halved

⅓ cup shredded Parmesan cheese

1. Preheat the oven to 350°F. Line a 12-muffin tin with 10 paper liners and coat with cooking spray.

2. In a medium skillet over medium heat, heat the olive oil until shimmering. Add the garlic and cook until fragrant, 30 seconds. Add the spinach and allow to gently wilt, using a spatula to fold the spinach over continuously, about 3 minutes. Remove the skillet from the heat and set aside to cool.

3. In a medium bowl, whisk together the eggs, water, and salt until well blended.

4. Add about 1 tablespoon of cooked spinach and 4 cherry tomato halves into each muffin cup. Evenly pour the egg mixture over the vegetables to fill the cup to just below the rim. Top with 1 heaping teaspoon of Parmesan.

5. Bake for about 30 minutes until the tops of the frittatas are slightly golden and a toothpick inserted into the center of a frittata comes out clean. Remove the muffin tin from the oven and allow to cool for 10 minutes.

6. Into each of 5 resealable containers or bags, place 2 frittatas.

Storage: Place airtight containers in the refrigerator for up to 1 week. To freeze, place freezer-safe containers in the freezer for up to 2 months. To defrost, refrigerate overnight. To reheat, remove the paper liners and microwave 2 frittatas at a time, uncovered, on high for about 1 minute. Alternatively, reheat thawed frittatas in a preheated 350°F oven for 10 minutes.

TOBY'S TIP: For a spin on this dish, swap the tomatoes with chopped broccoli, bell peppers, or mushrooms.

Per Serving (2 frittatas): Calories: 190; Total Fat: 12g; Saturated Fat: 4g; Protein: 16g; Total Carbs: 4g; Fiber: 1g; Sugar: 2g; Sodium: 368mg

VEGGIE-LOVERS' MEATLOAF WITH BAKED SWEET POTATO

MAKES 8 SERVINGS

PREP TIME: 20 minutes   COOK TIME: 1 hour 50 minutes

Adding vegetables to your meatloaf makes it more flavorful and helps keep it moist. Of course, it's also a great way to help meet the recommended vegetable intake, a feat that only 10 percent of Americans accomplish each day! You can also use leftover veggies—try chopped mushrooms or broccoli or sautéed spinach—the possibilities are endless.

Nonstick cooking spray

4 large sweet potatoes

1 pound 90% lean ground beef

1 (15-ounce) can low-sodium brown lentils, rinsed and drained

2 carrots, shredded

1 medium zucchini, shredded

1 medium onion, chopped

2 garlic cloves, minced

1 cup Meal Prep Barbecue Sauce (page 90), divided

1 cup gluten-free quick-cooking oats

1 large egg, beaten

½ teaspoon salt

¼ teaspoon freshly ground black pepper

1.   Preheat the oven to 400°F. Coat a baking sheet and a 9-by-5-inch loaf pan with cooking spray.

2.   Pierce each sweet potato several times with a fork. Place on the prepared baking sheet and bake until tender, about 50 minutes.

3.   Meanwhile, in a large bowl, combine the ground beef, lentils, carrots, zucchini, onion, garlic, ¼ cup of Meal Prep Barbecue Sauce, the oats, egg, salt, and pepper. Using clean hands, mix together well.

4.   Place the meat mixture into the prepared loaf pan, making sure the top is level. Pour the remaining ¾ cup of Meal Prep Barbecue Sauce over the meatloaf, using a spatula or the back of a wooden spoon to spread it evenly.

5.   Remove the sweet potatoes from the oven and set aside to cool for at least 10 minutes before slicing lengthwise. Reduce the oven temperature to 350°F.

6.   Bake the meatloaf for about 1 hour, until a thermometer inserted into the center of the meatloaf reads 155°F.

7. Remove from the oven, and allow to cool for 10 to 15 minutes before cutting into 8 equal slices.

8. Into each of 8 containers, place 1 slice of meatloaf with ½ baked sweet potato on the side. Store 4 containers in the refrigerator and freeze the remaining 4 for later.

Storage: Place airtight containers in the refrigerator for up to 1 week. To freeze, place freezer-safe containers in the freezer for up to 2 months. To defrost, refrigerate overnight. To reheat, microwave uncovered on high for 2 to 3 minutes.

> **TOBY'S TIP:** For a quick and easy side for meals or as a snack, bake sweet or russet potatoes as listed in steps 1 and 2 above. Make extras and store covered in the refrigerator for up to 7 days.

Per Serving (1 container): Calories: 464; Total Fat: 11g; Saturated Fat: 4g; Protein: 28g; Total Carbs: 65g; Fiber: 12g; Sugar: 20g; Sodium: 873mg

ROSEMARY–HONEY MUSTARD PORK TENDERLOIN WITH LEMON-DILL CARROTS

MAKES 4 SERVINGS

Good!

PREP TIME: 15 minutes, plus 30 minutes marinating time   **COOK TIME:** 1 hour

Did you know that pork tenderloin is just as lean as skinless, boneless chicken breast? This cut of pork meets the government guidelines for "extra lean." Enjoy this tasty dish without guilt—it's as good tasting as it is good for you.

¼ cup olive oil

2 tablespoons Dijon mustard

2 tablespoons honey

1 shallot, finely chopped

2 tablespoons coarsely chopped fresh rosemary

½ teaspoon salt

¼ teaspoon freshly ground black pepper

1¼ pounds boneless pork tenderloin, fat trimmed

Nonstick cooking spray

4 servings (2 cups) Lemon-Dill Carrots (page 149)

4 servings (3 cups) Brown Rice with Lentils (page 142)

1.   In a medium bowl, whisk together the olive oil, mustard, honey, shallot, rosemary, salt, and pepper. Add the pork to the bowl and turn to evenly coat. Cover the bowl and refrigerate for at least 30 minutes and up to overnight.

2.   Preheat the oven to 400°F.

3.   Place the pork tenderloin on a baking sheet, discarding the excess marinade. Cook until a thermometer inserted into the thickest part of the loin reads 145°F, about 40 minutes. Let the pork rest for 10 minutes before thinly slicing.

4.   Into each of 4 containers, place 2 or 3 slices of pork (about 4 ounces), ½ cup of Lemon-Dill Carrots, and ¾ cup of Brown Rice with Lentils.

Storage: Place airtight containers in the refrigerator for up to 1 week. To freeze, place freezer-safe containers in the freezer for up to 2 months. To defrost, refrigerate overnight. To reheat, microwave uncovered on high for 2 to 3 minutes.

TOBY'S TIP: Herbed Quinoa (page 140) and Zucchini Noodles with Lemon Vinaigrette (page 146) can be substituted for the Brown Rice with Lentils in this recipe.

Per Serving (1 container): Calories: 594; Total Fat: 26g; Saturated Fat: 4g; Protein: 37g; Total Carbs: 54g; Fiber: 10g; Sugar: 15g; Sodium: 757mg

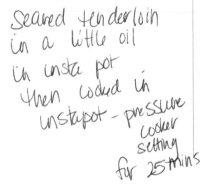

Seared tenderloin in a little oil in insta pot then cooked in instapot - pressure cooker setting for 25 mins.

CHOCOLATE PUDDING WITH RASPBERRIES

MAKES 5 PUDDINGS

PREP TIME: 10 minutes, plus at least 4 hours chill time   COOK TIME: 10 minutes

Most folks don't get the recommended three servings of milk and dairy per day. Milk provides nine essential nutrients, three of which, according to the Dietary Guidelines for Americans, are underconsumed by most Americans. These lacking but vital nutrients include vitamin D, potassium, and calcium, all of which are found in milk and other dairy foods. Here's a sweet way to get those numbers up!

2⅓ cups reduced-fat (2%) milk

1 tablespoon coconut oil

¼ cup 100% pure maple syrup

¼ cup unsweetened cocoa powder

1 teaspoon vanilla extract

⅛ teaspoon salt

¼ cup water

2 tablespoons cornstarch

1¼ cups fresh raspberries

1. In a medium saucepan over medium-low heat, heat the milk and coconut oil, stirring, until the oil is melted. Add the maple syrup, cocoa powder, vanilla, and salt, and stir to incorporate.

2. In a small bowl, whisk together the water and cornstarch. Add to the saucepan and whisk to blend. Increase the heat to medium and cook, stirring regularly, until the pudding thickens, about 5 minutes. Remove the saucepan from the heat and set aside to slightly cool.

3. Divide the pudding into each of 5 containers (about ½ cup each) and place plastic wrap over the pudding (make sure the plastic is touching the pudding). Cover and refrigerate for at least 4 hours and then remove the plastic wrap and top each pudding with ¼ cup of raspberries.

Storage: Place airtight containers in the refrigerator for up to 5 days.

TOBY'S TIP: Want your chocolate pudding even chocolatier? Melt 1 or 2 ounces of 60- to 70-percent dark chocolate in the microwave and add it to the pudding in step 1 with the maple syrup.

Per Serving (1 container): Calories: 169; Total Fat: 6g; Saturated Fat: 4g; Protein: 5g; Total Carbs: 25g; Fiber: 3g; Sugar: 18g; Sodium: 115mg

MEAL PREP 6

THIS WEEK IT'S ALL ABOUT using herbs and spices to boost flavor. Herbs and spices are low in calories and provide small amounts of vitamins, minerals, and phytochemicals (natural plant compounds that help prevent and fight disease). There will likely be a handful of spices that you'll need to stock in your pantry, but once you make this meal prep regularly, you'll get your money's worth.

You'll also find a surprising snack: Double Chocolate Black Bean Brownies. Although your typical brownie is high in calories, added sugar, and saturated fat, these babies are filled with protein, fiber, and lots of vitamins and minerals. You won't believe how tasty they are!

≪ Grilled Chicken with Carrot-Cabbage Slaw (page 74)

SHOPPING LIST

PANTRY

- Baking powder
- Beans, black, low-sodium, (2 [15-ounce] cans)
- Black pepper, freshly ground
- Broth, low-sodium vegetable (1 [32-ounce] container)
- Canola oil
- Cardamom, ground
- Chiles, diced green (1 [4-ounce] can)
- Chili powder
- Chocolate, dark, 60% to 70% cacao (2 ounces)
- Cocoa powder, unsweetened
- Coconut, unsweetened shredded
- Coffee, instant
- Couscous, whole-wheat
- Cumin, ground
- Flour, all-purpose, unbleached
- Flour, white 100% whole-wheat
- Garlic powder
- Honey
- Maple syrup, 100% pure
- Mustard powder
- Nonstick cooking spray
- Oats, old-fashioned
- Olive oil
- Onion powder
- Oregano, dried
- Paprika, ground
- Paprika, smoked, ground
- Peanut butter, smooth
- Quinoa
- Salt
- Sugar, granulated
- Thyme, dried
- Tomatoes, diced, no salt added (1 [14.5-ounce] can)
- Vanilla extract

FRUIT, VEGETABLES, HERBS & SPICES

- Banana, medium (1)
- Basil (1 bunch)
- Broccoli florets (1-pound bag)
- Cabbage, red or green (4 cups pre-shredded or 1 head)
- Carrots (1 bunch)
- Garlic (1 head)
- Lemons (3)
- Onion, yellow (1)
- Parsley (1 bunch)
- Peppers, red or other color (5 large)
- Pineapple (1)
- Scallion (1 bunch)
- Strawberries (1 [16-ounce] container)

PROTEIN

- Chicken breast, skinless, boneless (4 [5-ounce] breasts)
- Chicken tenders, skinless, boneless (10 ounces)
- Eggs, large (4)

DAIRY

- Greek yogurt, nonfat plain (1 [32-ounce] container)
- Milk, nonfat (1 quart)
- Pepper Jack cheese, shredded (3 ounces)

FROZEN

- Corn, frozen yellow kernels (10-ounce package)

	BREAKFAST	LUNCH	DINNER	SNACK
DAY 1	Tropical Overnight Oats	Grilled Chicken with Carrot-Cabbage Slaw	Mexican-Style Stuffed Peppers	Double Chocolate Black Bean Brownies
DAY 2	Whole-Grain Pancakes with Peanut Butter– Maple Drizzle	Grilled Chicken with Carrot-Cabbage Slaw	Mexican-Style Stuffed Peppers	Double Chocolate Black Bean Brownies
DAY 3	Tropical Overnight Oats	Chicken Shawarma Bowl	Grilled Chicken with Carrot-Cabbage Slaw	Double Chocolate Black Bean Brownies
DAY 4	Whole-Grain Pancakes with Peanut Butter– Maple Drizzle	Grilled Chicken with Carrot-Cabbage Slaw	Mexican-Style Stuffed Peppers	Double Chocolate Black Bean Brownies
DAY 5	Whole-Grain Pancakes with Peanut Butter– Maple Drizzle	Chicken Shawarma Bowl	Mexican-Style Stuffed Peppers	Double Chocolate Black Bean Brownies

EQUIPMENT

- 8-by-8-inch baking dish
- Baking sheet
- Chef's knife
- Cutting board
- Measuring cups and spoons
- Mixing bowls
- Saucepans
- Skillet
- Steamer basket

STEP-BY-STEP PREP

1.   Prepare the **Tropical Overnight Oats** (page 71) through step 1, and prep all the fruit.

2.   Prepare the **Mexican-Style Stuffed Peppers** (page 76) through step 1.

3.   While the quinoa is cooking, prepare the **Herb-Yogurt Dressing** (page 87). When the quinoa is cooked, set it aside to cool.

CONTINUED ▶

4.   Preheat the oven to 350°F, and put the **Mexican-Style Stuffed Peppers** in the oven to cook for 50 minutes, step 5 (first part) (page 77).

5.   While the stuffed peppers cook, fully prepare the **Grilled Chicken with Carrot-Cabbage Slaw** (page 74).

6.   Fully prepare the **Whole-Grain Pancakes with Peanut Butter–Maple Drizzle** (page 72).

7.   Uncover the **Mexican-Style Stuffed Peppers** and continue cooking for 20 minutes, step 5 (second part) (page 77).

8.   Prepare the **Chicken Shawarma Bowl** (page 78) through step 1. While the chicken marinates, prepare the **Double Chocolate Black Bean Brownies**, step 5 (but do not put in the oven yet) (page 79).

9.   Once the stuffed peppers are cooked, remove them from the oven. Place the brownies in the oven to bake for 25 minutes to complete step 5.

10. Prepare the **Parsleyed Whole-Wheat Couscous** through step 2 (page 144).

11. Remove the chicken from the refrigerator and continue preparing the **Chicken Shawarma Bowl**, steps 2 through 5 (page 78). Complete the stuffed peppers, step 6.

12. Remove the brownies from the oven when cooked, and follow step 6 of the recipe.

TROPICAL OVERNIGHT OATS

MAKES 2 SERVINGS

PREP TIME: 10 minutes, plus 8 to 10 hours to chill

Christopher Columbus introduced pineapple to Europe after he discovered them in the Caribbean. Today, Hawaii is the leading producer of this fruit. Pineapple provides a healthy dose of nutrients—just 1 cup contains 2 grams of fiber and 131 percent of your daily vitamin C. It also provides 76 percent of your daily manganese for good bone health. This fruit also has a protein-digesting enzyme called bromelain, which helps fight inflammation in the body.

1 cup gluten-free old-fashioned oats, divided

¼ cup unsweetened shredded coconut, divided

⅔ cup nonfat milk or light coconut milk, divided

2 tablespoons 100% pure maple syrup, divided

1 cup diced fresh pineapple

1 cup sliced strawberries

1. Into each of two 12-ounce jars, place ½ cup of oats, 2 tablespoons of shredded coconut, ⅓ cup of milk, and 1 tablespoon of maple syrup; stir to blend. Cover the jars and refrigerate overnight.

2. Stir to recombine the mixture. Add ½ cup each of pineapple and strawberries on the side of the jar. Top with the fruit right before eating or before grabbing and going.

Storage: Place covered jars in the refrigerator for up to 3 days. If you choose to warm the oats, heat uncovered in the microwave for 2 minutes, then add the fruit.

TOBY'S TIP: Switch up or add kiwi, mango, and guava to this tropical delight.

Per Serving (1 jar): Calories: 358; Total Fat: 10g; Saturated Fat: 7g; Protein: 9g; Total Carbs: 63g; Fiber: 7g; Sugar: 30g; Sodium: 42mg

WHOLE-GRAIN PANCAKES WITH PEANUT BUTTER– MAPLE DRIZZLE

MAKES 6 SERVINGS

PREP TIME: 15 minutes   **COOK TIME:** 25 minutes

Most folks top their pancakes with maple syrup, but this unique version combines peanut butter with maple syrup for a truly mouthwatering drizzle. Plus, the peanut butter offers a boost of protein and healthy fat that will keep you satisfied throughout your busy morning.

FOR THE PANCAKES

1 cup unbleached all-purpose flour

1 cup 100% white whole-wheat flour or 100% whole-wheat flour

1 tablespoon baking powder

½ teaspoon salt

1 cup nonfat milk

½ cup nonfat plain Greek yogurt

3 tablespoons granulated sugar

1½ tablespoons canola oil

2 large eggs, beaten

1 teaspoon vanilla extract

Nonstick cooking spray

1. In a medium bowl, sift together the all-purpose flour, whole-wheat flour, baking powder, and salt.

2. In another medium bowl, whisk together the milk, Greek yogurt, sugar, oil, eggs, and vanilla. Fold the dry ingredients into the wet ingredients until just combined. Do not overmix.

3. Coat a griddle or large skillet with cooking spray and place over medium heat. Once hot, scoop a heaping ¼ cup of batter onto the griddle. Repeat, leaving room between the pancakes. Cook until the tops are bubbly and the edges set, 3 to 4 minutes. Flip the pancakes over and cook until golden brown and crisp along the edges, about 2 minutes. Remove from the heat and keep warm until ready to serve. Repeat with the remaining batter.

FOR THE DRIZZLE

¼ cup smooth peanut butter

½ cup 100% pure
   maple syrup

1 teaspoon vanilla extract

4. To make the drizzle, put the peanut butter, maple syrup, and vanilla in a small saucepan and bring to a boil. Reduce the heat and simmer, whisking occasionally, until the flavors combine, about 5 minutes. Set aside to cool.

5. Into each of 6 containers, place 2 pancakes. Into each of 6 microwave-safe small jars or containers, pour 2 tablespoons of drizzle.

Storage: Place the pancakes and drizzle in separate airtight containers in the refrigerator for up to 1 week. To freeze, place the pancakes only in a freezer-safe container in the freezer for up to 2 months. To defrost, refrigerate overnight. To reheat, microwave uncovered pancakes for about 30 seconds, and do the same with the drizzle. Top the pancakes with the drizzle before eating.

TOBY'S TIP: Make these blueberry pancakes by adding 1 cup of fresh blueberries to the batter before cooking.

Per Serving (1 pancake with 2 tablespoons sauce): Calories: 375; Total Fat: 11g; Saturated Fat: 2g; Protein: 12g; Total Carbs: 59g; Fiber: 3g; Sugar: 29g; Sodium: 443mg

GRILLED CHICKEN WITH CARROT-CABBAGE SLAW

MAKES 4 SERVINGS

PREP TIME: 20 minutes   COOK TIME: 30 minutes

Cabbage is a member of the mustard family, which also includes Brussels sprouts, cauliflower, and kale. This veggie is a good source of vitamin C and fiber. Red cabbage also contains anthocyanins, plant chemicals that act as powerful antioxidants. Studies have linked cabbage and other members of the mustard family to helping prevent cancer.

FOR THE CHICKEN

1 tablespoon garlic powder

1 tablespoon onion powder

1 tablespoon dried thyme

1 tablespoon ground paprika

1 teaspoon mustard powder

¼ teaspoon salt

Nonstick cooking spray

4 (5-ounce) skinless, boneless chicken breasts

FOR THE SLAW

4 cups shredded red or green cabbage (about 1 small head)

4 medium carrots, trimmed, peeled, and shredded

4 servings (½ cup) Herb-Yogurt Dressing (page 87)

1.   Preheat the oven to 375°F.

2.   In a small bowl, combine the garlic powder, onion powder, thyme, paprika, mustard powder, and salt. Using clean hands, pat the dry rub over both sides of the chicken breasts.

3.   Preheat a grill or grill pan coated with cooking spray over medium-high heat. Add the chicken breasts and cook, flipping once, until browned on both sides, about 15 minutes.

4.   Transfer the chicken to an 8-by-8-inch baking dish and place in the oven for about 15 minutes until the chicken reaches a minimum internal cooking temperature of 165°F. Set the chicken aside to cool. Once cooled, slice each chicken breast into thin strips.

5.   To make the slaw, mix together the shredded cabbage and carrots in a medium bowl. Add the Herb-Yogurt Dressing and toss to combine.

6.   Into each of 4 containers, place 2 cups of slaw and top with 1 sliced chicken breast.

Storage: Place airtight containers in the refrigerator for up to 5 days. To freeze, place the chicken only in freezer-safe containers for up to 2 months. To defrost, refrigerate overnight. The chicken can be eaten cold with the slaw. Alternatively, reheat individual servings uncovered in the microwave on high for about 45 seconds.

> **TOBY'S TIP:** Tougher vegetables like cabbage and carrots get less soggy in the refrigerator and are perfect for meal prepping. The Herb-Yogurt Dressing helps add flavor and also softens the veggies to perfection.

Per Serving (1 container): Calories: 263; Total Fat: 6g; Saturated Fat: 1g; Protein: 37g; Total Carbs: 15g; Fiber: 5g; Sugar: 7g; Sodium: 302mg

MEXICAN-STYLE STUFFED PEPPERS

MAKES 5 SERVINGS

PREP TIME: 15 minutes   **COOK TIME:** 1 hour 40 minutes

Red peppers are brimming with good-for-you nutrients. One large red pepper contains just 51 calories, and 350 percent of your recommended daily vitamin C! It's also a good source of fiber and vitamins A, K, and B6. The red peppers have more beta-carotene and vitamin E than the green ones. Peppers are also packed with plant compounds including lycopene, an antioxidant that helps lower the risk of heart disease, prostate cancer, and macular degeneration (an eye disease associated with aging).

½ cup quinoa

1 cup low-sodium vegetable broth or water

Nonstick cooking spray

1 tablespoon olive oil

1 small onion, chopped

1 garlic clove, minced

½ cup canned low-sodium black beans, rinsed and drained

¼ cup frozen corn kernels, defrosted

1 (14.5-ounce) can no-salt-added diced tomatoes

1 (4-ounce) can diced green chiles

1 teaspoon chili powder

¼ teaspoon smoked paprika

¼ teaspoon dried oregano

¼ teaspoon salt

⅛ teaspoon ground cumin

⅛ teaspoon freshly ground black pepper

1.   In a medium saucepan, bring the quinoa and broth to a boil over high heat. Reduce the heat to low, cover, and simmer until all the liquid is absorbed, 12 to 15 minutes. Remove from the heat and fluff the quinoa with a fork.

2.   Preheat the oven to 350°F. Coat a large baking dish with cooking spray.

3.   In a medium skillet over medium heat, heat the oil. Add the onion and garlic, and cook until the onion is translucent and the garlic is fragrant, about 3 minutes. Add the black beans and corn, and toss to combine. Add the tomatoes, chiles, chili powder, paprika, oregano, salt, cumin, and black pepper. Bring the mixture to a boil and then reduce the heat and simmer, stirring occasionally, for about 10 minutes. Add the cooked quinoa and stir to combine. Set the mixture aside to slightly cool.

4.   Slice the tops off the peppers. Using a paring knife, remove the membranes and seeds. Spoon ¾ cup of the quinoa mixture into each pepper, and arrange the peppers in the prepared baking dish, leaving about 2 inches between them. Top each pepper with 2 tablespoons of shredded cheese. Cover the dish loosely with aluminum foil.

5 large red, yellow, orange, or green bell peppers

10 tablespoons shredded Pepper Jack cheese, divided

5. Bake for 50 minutes. Uncover and continue baking for an additional 20 minutes. Remove from the oven and set aside to slightly cool.

6. Place each stuffed pepper in a container, cover, and refrigerate.

Storage: Place airtight containers in the refrigerator for up to 1 week. To freeze, place freezer-safe containers in the freezer for up to 2 months. To defrost, refrigerate overnight. To reheat, microwave uncovered on high for 1½ to 2 minutes.

TOBY'S TIP: You can also stuff heirloom tomatoes. Slice the tops off and scoop out the insides, add the stuffing, and cook for about 25 to 30 minutes.

Per Serving (1 container): Calories: 255; Total Fat: 9g; Saturated Fat: 3g; Protein: 10g; Total Carbs: 34g; Fiber: 8g; Sugar: 11g; Sodium: 377mg

CHICKEN SHAWARMA BOWL

MAKES 2 SERVINGS

PREP TIME: 20 minutes, plus 20 minutes marinating time　　COOK TIME: 15 minutes

Shawarma is traditionally served in the Middle East and is usually made with lamb cooked on a revolving spit and shaved with a sharp knife for serving. This version uses chicken flavored with a combo of low-calorie spices and is grilled—no revolving spit needed here!

1 tablespoon olive oil

Juice of 1 lemon

½ teaspoon garlic powder

½ teaspoon onion powder

½ teaspoon ground cardamom

½ teaspoon ground cumin

½ teaspoon smoked paprika

¼ teaspoon salt

⅛ teaspoon freshly ground black pepper

10 ounces boneless, skinless chicken tenders

Nonstick cooking spray

3 cups broccoli florets

2 servings (1 cup) Parsleyed Whole-Wheat Couscous (page 144)

1. In a medium bowl, whisk together the oil, lemon juice, garlic powder, onion powder, cardamom, cumin, paprika, salt, and pepper. Place the chicken in the marinade and toss to coat. Cover and place in the refrigerator for at least 20 minutes and up to overnight.

2. Coat a sauté or grill pan with cooking spray and put over medium heat. When the oil is shimmering, add the chicken tenders and cook 10 to 12 minutes, turning once, until they reach a minimum internal cooking temperature of 165°F. Discard the excess marinade.

3. Remove the chicken breasts from the heat and set aside to cool.

4. Fill a medium saucepan with 1 inch of water. Insert a fitter steamer basket, place the broccoli florets inside, and cover. Bring the water to a boil, reduce the heat to medium, and steam the broccoli for 5 minutes. Immediately remove the broccoli from the saucepan and set aside to cool.

5. Into each of 2 resealable containers, place ½ cup of Parsleyed Whole-Wheat Couscous side by side with 1½ cups of broccoli, and top with 1 sliced chicken breast.

Storage: Place airtight containers in the refrigerator for up to 1 week. To reheat, microwave uncovered on high for 2 minutes.

TOBY'S TIP: Serve this bowl alongside Simple Hummus with Vegetables (page 152).

Per Serving (1 container): Calories: 390; Total Fat: 15g; Saturated Fat: 2g; Protein: 37g; Total Carbs: 31g; Fiber: 3g; Sugar: 2g; Sodium: 610mg

DOUBLE CHOCOLATE BLACK BEAN BROWNIES

MAKES 8 BROWNIES

PREP TIME: 15 minutes   **COOK TIME:** 30 minutes

These brownies are made without any flour and come out supersoft. Although you may not be used to making brownies with beans, they provide a ton of nutrients including protein, fiber, iron, calcium, and zinc. You won't taste *any* beans; the chocolate, coffee, and banana overpower the flavor.

Nonstick cooking spray

1 (15-ounce) can low-sodium black beans, rinsed and drained

1 medium banana, mashed

½ cup 100% pure maple syrup

2 eggs, beaten

2 tablespoons canola or grapeseed oil

1 teaspoon vanilla extract

⅓ cup unsweetened cocoa powder

1 tablespoon instant coffee

½ teaspoon baking powder

¼ teaspoon salt

2 ounces dark chocolate (60% to 70% cacao)

1. Preheat the oven to 350°F. Coat an 8-inch-by-8-inch baking dish with cooking spray.

2. Place the black beans in a blender and blend until smooth. Add the mashed banana, maple syrup, eggs, oil, and vanilla, and blend well.

3. Add the cocoa powder, instant coffee, baking powder, and salt and blend to incorporate.

4. In a microwave-safe bowl, microwave the dark chocolate until melted, stirring every 30 seconds, about 1½ minutes. Allow to slightly cool for a few minutes, then add to the blender and blend well.

5. Pour the brownie mixture into the prepared baking dish. Bake for about 25 minutes until a toothpick inserted into the center comes out clean.

6. Remove the baking dish from the oven and allow to cool for at least 10 minutes before cutting into 8 brownies. Wrap individually or place in a resealable container.

Storage: Store brownies at room temperature for up to 5 days. To freeze, place freezer-safe container in the freezer for up to 2 months. Defrost at room temperature. Eat at room temperature or reheat from thawed in a 350°F oven for 10 minutes to warm.

Per Serving (1 brownie): Calories: 218; Total Fat: 8g; Saturated Fat: 2g; Protein: 6g; Total Carbs: 32g; Fiber: 5g; Sugar: 18g; Sodium: 198mg

PART TWO

BONUS MEAL PREP RECIPES

STAPLES & SAUCES

◄◄ Meal Prep Salsa (page 91)

GREEN GODDESS DRESSING

MAKES 1 CUP

PREP TIME: 10 minutes

Traditionally, this dressing is made with a combination of low-calorie herbs. This version uses avocado, which adds healthy fats, numerous vitamins and minerals, plus a creamy consistency. Avocados also provide the carotenoids lutein and zeaxanthin, which are shown to keep the eyes healthy and may help reduce the risk of macular degeneration, the leading cause of vision loss as we age.

1 Hass avocado

1 garlic clove

1 scallion, sliced

½ cup roughly chopped fresh parsley

½ cup roughly chopped fresh basil

1 tablespoon freshly squeezed lemon juice

1 teaspoon anchovy paste

⅛ teaspoon freshly ground black pepper

3 tablespoons nonfat plain Greek yogurt

3 tablespoons light mayonnaise

In a blender, process the avocado, garlic, scallion, parsley, basil, lemon juice, anchovy paste, pepper, yogurt, and mayonnaise together until smooth.

Storage: Store in a resealable container in the refrigerator for up to 1 week.

TOBY'S TIP: To make an anchovy-free version, replace the anchovy paste with ¼ teaspoon salt.

Per Serving (2 tablespoons): Calories: 62; Total Fat: 5g; Saturated Fat: 1g; Protein: 1g; Total Carbs: 4g; Fiber: 2g; Sugar: 1g; Sodium: 100mg

LEMON-BALSAMIC VINAIGRETTE

MAKES 1 CUP

PREP TIME: 10 minutes

Eliminate all those salad dressing bottles in your refrigerator! Homemade dressings are the simplest recipes to whip up with ingredients you already have sitting in your pantry. There are also no preservatives and additives, since you are in control of the ingredients.

3 tablespoons balsamic vinegar

2 tablespoons freshly squeezed lemon juice

1 teaspoon gluten-free Dijon mustard

½ teaspoon salt

¼ teaspoon freshly ground black pepper

⅔ cup extra-virgin olive oil

In a small bowl, whisk together the balsamic vinegar, lemon juice, mustard, salt, and pepper. Slowly drizzle the olive oil into the mixture, whisking to incorporate.

Storage: Store in an airtight container in the refrigerator for up to 2 weeks.

TOBY'S TIP: To make traditional balsamic vinaigrette, replace the lemon juice with balsamic vinegar, for a total of 5 tablespoons vinegar.

Per Serving (2 tablespoons): Calories: 166; Total Fat: 19g; Saturated Fat: 3g; Protein: 0g; Total Carbs: 1g; Fiber: 0g; Sugar: 1g; Sodium: 163mg

KICKIN' RANCH DRESSING

MAKES 1¼ CUPS

PREP TIME: 10 minutes, plus at least 30 minutes chill time

A tasty, light dressing pairs perfectly with salads and cut-up veggies for a healthy snack. This version of a lighter ranch dressing uses Greek yogurt and buttermilk, which provide the good nutrients found in dairy foods, including protein, phosphorus, calcium, vitamins A and D, riboflavin, niacin, and pantothenic acid.

½ cup low-fat buttermilk

6 tablespoons reduced-fat (2%) plain Greek yogurt

¼ cup reduced-fat mayonnaise

2 tablespoons finely chopped flat-leaf parsley

1 tablespoon finely chopped fresh dill

1 tablespoon finely chopped fresh chives

Juice of ½ lemon (about 1 tablespoon)

1 garlic clove, roughly chopped

½ teaspoon salt

¼ teaspoon freshly ground black pepper

⅛ teaspoon cayenne pepper

⅛ teaspoon smoked paprika

1. In a blender, process the buttermilk, yogurt, mayonnaise, parsley, dill, chives, lemon juice, garlic, salt, black pepper, cayenne, and paprika together until smooth.

2. Transfer the dressing to a container, cover, and refrigerate for at least 30 minutes before using.

Storage: Store in an airtight container in the refrigerator for up to 1 week.

TOBY'S TIP: To add even more spice to the dressing, add ¼ to ½ teaspoon of Sriracha.

Per Serving (2 tablespoons): Calories: 26; Total Fat: 1g; Saturated Fat: 0g; Protein: 1g; Total Carbs: 2g; Fiber: 0g; Sugar: 1g; Sodium: 194mg

HERB-YOGURT DRESSING

MAKES 1¼ CUPS

PREP TIME: 15 minutes

Herbs offer a delicious, low-calorie way to flavor dressings, plus they contribute vital nutrients. Basil and parsley are brimming with the antioxidants vitamins A and C, as well as vitamin K. Parsley also contains small amounts of folate, potassium, calcium, and iron.

1 cup nonfat plain Greek yogurt

½ cup fresh basil leaves, roughly chopped

½ cup fresh parsley, roughly chopped

1 scallion, roughly chopped

1 tablespoon canola oil

1 tablespoon freshly squeezed lemon juice

1 teaspoon honey

¼ teaspoon salt

1. In a blender, process the yogurt, basil, parsley, scallion, oil, lemon juice, honey, and salt together until smooth.

2. Transfer the dressing to a container, cover, and refrigerate for at least 30 minutes before using.

Storage: Store in an airtight container in the refrigerator for up to 1 week.

TOBY'S TIP: Use whatever leftover herbs are sitting in your refrigerator—mint, chives, and rosemary can all get the trick done!

Per Serving (2 tablespoons) Calories: 30; Total Fat: 2g; Saturated Fat: 0g; Protein: 2g; Total Carbs: 2g; Fiber: 0g; Sugar: 1g; Sodium: 69mg

CHILE-GARLIC SAUCE

MAKES ¾ CUP

PREP TIME: 10 minutes

When making sauces or dressings with Asian flavors, oftentimes a touch of sweetness needs to be added to balance the savory umami flavor. I typically use honey, which has been shown to have numerous health benefits. Research suggests that honey helps gut health by feeding good bacteria. Plus, honey contains a wide variety of natural plant chemicals, including flavonoids and phenolic acids, that can help prevent and fight disease. Both these natural plant chemicals have been shown to act as antioxidants.

1 (4-ounce) can diced red or green chiles

4 garlic cloves

2 tablespoons toasted sesame oil

1½ teaspoons honey

2 tablespoons unseasoned rice vinegar

¼ teaspoon salt

In a blender, process the chiles, garlic, oil, honey, rice vinegar, and salt together until smooth.

Storage: Store in an airtight container in the refrigerator for up to 1 week.

TOBY'S TIP: Diced red or green chiles can be found in the Mexican foods section of your supermarket.

Per Serving (about 2½ tablespoons): Calories: 78; Total Fat: 7g; Saturated Fat: 1g; Protein: 0g; Total Carbs: 4g; Fiber: 1g; Sugar: 2g; Sodium: 261mg

CHUNKY TOMATO SAUCE

MAKES 5 CUPS

PREP TIME: 10 minutes   COOK TIME: 20 minutes

Canned tomatoes contain a wide variety of nutrients, including vitamins C and E, potassium, and fiber. They're also loaded with powerful antioxidants such as beta-carotene and lycopene. Tomatoes are cooked during the canning process, and lycopene has been found to be more absorbable by the body in its cooked form. Therefore, canned tomatoes actually have more of the cancer-fighting lycopene benefits than the raw variety.

2 tablespoons olive oil

5 garlic cloves, minced

1 (28-ounce) can whole peeled plum tomatoes

1 (28-ounce) can crushed tomatoes

½ teaspoon salt

¼ teaspoon freshly ground black pepper

½ cup basil leaves, cut into thin strips

In a medium pot over medium heat, heat the oil until it shimmers. Add the garlic and cook until fragrant, about 1 minute. Add the whole and crushed tomatoes, cover, and bring to a boil. Reduce the heat and simmer, covered, for 20 minutes, breaking up the tomatoes as they cook. Stir in the salt, pepper, and basil.

Storage: Store in airtight containers in the refrigerator for up to 1 week. To freeze, place in freezer-safe containers for up to 3 months. Defrost in the refrigerator overnight. Reheat individual portions uncovered in the microwave on high for 1 to 2 minutes. Alternatively, reheat the entire batch in a medium pot on the stove top. Bring to a boil then reduce the heat and simmer until heated through, about 10 minutes.

> **TOBY'S TIP:** Like a smooth sauce? Pour the tomato sauce into your blender or use an immersion blender and blend until smooth.

Per Serving (½ cup): Calories: 66; Total Fat: 3g; Saturated Fat: 0g; Protein: 2g; Total Carbs: 9g; Fiber: 3g; Sugar: 5g; Sodium: 521mg

MEAL PREP BARBECUE SAUCE | MAKES 1½ CUPS

PREP TIME: 10 minutes

Many store-bought varieties of barbecue sauce have more sugar than is necessary, so make your own—you then control the ingredients, and you can mix it up to your preferences. This recipe contains ingredients you probably already have in the house, so you'll never again be caught without 'cue sauce on hand!

1½ cups ketchup

8 teaspoons apple cider vinegar

¼ cup brown sugar

2 tablespoons Worcestershire sauce

2 garlic cloves, minced

1 tablespoon smoked paprika

¼ teaspoon salt

In a small bowl, whisk together the ketchup, vinegar, brown sugar, Worcestershire sauce, garlic, paprika, and salt.

Storage: Store in an airtight container in the refrigerator for up to 2 weeks.

TOBY'S TIP: Want more smokiness in your barbecue sauce? Add 1 or 2 more teaspoons of smoked paprika.

Per Serving (2 tablespoons): Calories: 50; Total Fat: 0g; Saturated Fat: 0g; Protein: 0g; Total Carbs: 12g; Fiber: 0g; Sugar: 10g; Sodium: 351mg

MEAL PREP SALSA

MAKES 4 CUPS

PREP TIME: 10 minutes

Salsa is the perfect condiment for meal prep purposes. You can add it to eggs, chicken, quinoa, potatoes, and more! Plus, salsa is lower in calories with just 24 per ¼ cup serving. It is an excellent source of the antioxidant vitamins A and C, and a good source of folate, vitamin B6, thiamin, and potassium.

1 pound plum tomatoes, chopped (4 or 5)

1 green bell pepper, chopped

½ medium onion, chopped

2 garlic cloves, minced

1 jalapeño pepper, seeded and chopped

¼ cup chopped fresh cilantro

2 tablespoons freshly squeezed lime juice (about 1 lime)

2 tablespoons extra-virgin olive oil

½ teaspoon salt

¼ teaspoon freshly ground black pepper

In a medium bowl, mix together the tomatoes, bell pepper, onion, garlic, jalapeño, and cilantro. Add the lime juice, oil, salt, and black pepper, and mix to evenly coat.

Storage: Store in an airtight container in the refrigerator for up to 1 week.

TOBY'S TIP: Want a spicier salsa? Leave the seeds in the jalapeño for that extra bite.

Per Serving (¼ cup): Calories: 24: Total Fat: 2g; Saturated Fat: 0g; Protein: 0g; Total Carbs: 2g; Fiber: 1g; Sugar: 1g; Sodium: 76mg

BREAKFAST

« Blackberry Bran Muffins (page 96)

SPINACH-BERRY SMOOTHIE PACKS

MAKES 5 SMOOTHIES

PREP TIME: 10 minutes

Smoothie packs contain all your smoothie ingredients, except the liquid, which you'll add right before blending. They help shave off a good five minutes from your morning routine and deliver a delicious on-the-go healthy breakfast!

10 cups baby spinach, washed and patted dry

2½ cups fresh or frozen strawberries

2½ cups fresh or frozen blueberries or blackberries

5 pitted dates

3¾ cups apple juice, divided

1.   Into each of 5 resealable plastic bags, put 2 cups of spinach, ½ cup of strawberries, ½ cup of blueberries, and 1 date. Seal the bags and freeze for at least 2 hours.

2.   When ready to make the smoothie, pour ¾ cup of apple juice into the blender. Add the contents of one smoothie pack and blend until smooth.

3.   Pour into a to-go cup and enjoy.

Storage: Freezer packs can be stored for up to 2 months. When ready to make the smoothie, use straight from the freezer.

TOBY'S TIP: Swap the spinach for the same amount of chopped kale.

Per Serving (16-fluid-ounce smoothie): Calories: 241; Total Fat: 0g; Saturated Fat: 0g; Protein: 3g; Total Carbs: 62g; Fiber: 7g; Sugar: 49g; Sodium: 98mg

MORNING SUNSHINE SMOOTHIE PACKS

MAKES 5 SMOOTHIES

PREP TIME: 10 minutes

When you think of a bright orange-yellow-hued smoothie, oranges, bananas, and pineapple probably come to mind. Yep, this smoothie contains all three, plus the added orange goodness of carrots, which provide vitamin A, fiber, potassium, and vitamins C and K. Vitamin A helps maintain good eyesight, which is probably why your mom always told you to eat your carrots!

5 medium bananas, cut into chunks

Zest of 1 orange, divided

5 medium carrots, shredded

2½ cups fresh sliced or frozen pineapple chunks

1 pitted date

3¾ cups nonfat milk, divided

1. Into each of 5 resealable plastic bags, put chunks of 1 banana, about ½ teaspoon of orange zest, 1 shredded carrot, ½ cup of pineapple, and 1 date. Seal the bags and freeze for at least 2 hours.

2. When ready to make the smoothie, pour ¾ cup of milk into the blender. Add the contents of one smoothie pack, and blend until smooth.

3. Pour into a to-go cup and enjoy.

Storage: Freezer packs can be stored for up to 2 months. When ready to make the smoothie, use straight from the freezer.

TOBY'S TIP: Swap the nonfat milk for almond milk or 100% orange juice to make this smoothie dairy-free.

Per Serving (24-fluid-ounce smoothie): Calories: 252; Total Fat: 1g; Saturated Fat: 0g; Protein: 10g; Total Carbs: 55g; Fiber: 6g; Sugar: 26g; Sodium: 153mg

BLACKBERRY BRAN MUFFINS

MAKES 12 MUFFINS

PREP TIME: 20 minutes   COOK TIME: 20 minutes

Muffins are one of the easiest foods to grab and go. Those oversized store-bought versions, however, can weigh in at close to 400 calories each! My equally satisfying version ups the whole grains and adds protein, with just over 200 calories each.

Nonstick cooking spray

2 cups whole-wheat flour or white whole-wheat flour

¼ cup oat bran

2 teaspoons baking powder

1 teaspoon baking soda

¼ teaspoon salt

½ cup light brown sugar

½ cup low-fat (1%) milk

½ cup olive oil or canola oil

1 cup reduced-fat (2%) plain Greek yogurt

1 large egg plus 1 large egg yolk

1 teaspoon vanilla extract

1½ cups fresh or frozen and thawed blackberries

¼ cup rolled oats, divided

1.   Preheat the oven to 375°F. Coat a 12-muffin tin with cooking spray and set aside.

2.   In a medium bowl, sift together the flour, oat bran, baking powder, baking soda, and salt.

3.   In a large bowl, whisk together the brown sugar, milk, and oil. Add the yogurt, egg, egg yolk, and vanilla. Whisk until smooth.

4.   Gently fold the dry ingredients into the wet ingredients, being careful not to overmix. Gently fold in the blackberries to evenly distribute them throughout the batter.

5.   Using a ¼-cup scoop, transfer the batter into the prepared muffin tin. Tap the muffin tin a few times on the counter to release any air bubbles. Sprinkle each muffin with 1 teaspoon of rolled oats. Bake for 20 minutes until golden brown and a toothpick inserted in the center comes out clean.

6.   Remove from the oven and allow to cool for 10 minutes before removing the muffins from the tin.

Storage: Place in an airtight container and keep at room temperature for up to 5 days. To freeze, place in a freezer-safe container or freezer bag for up to 2 months. Defrost at room temperature. Enjoy at room temperature or toast in a toaster oven.

TOBY'S TIP: Swap the blackberries for strawberries, blueberries, raspberries, or a combination, keeping the total amount at 1½ cups.

Per Serving (1 muffin): Calories: 217; Total Fat: 11g; Saturated Fat: 2g; Protein: 7g; Total Carbs: 26g; Fiber: 4g; Sugar: 8g; Sodium: 121mg

PEAR–PUMPKIN SEED MUFFINS

MAKES 12 MUFFINS

PREP TIME: 15 minutes   COOK TIME: 25 minutes

When you bake muffins at home, you can choose smart ingredients. These muffins combine sweet pears with savory pumpkin seeds.

Nonstick cooking spray

1 ¼ cups unbleached all-purpose flour

1 cup whole-wheat pastry flour

1 teaspoon baking powder

½ teaspoon baking soda

⅛ teaspoon salt

½ cup creamy almond or sunflower seed butter, at room temperature

½ cup nonfat plain Greek yogurt

½ cup low-fat (1%) milk

½ cup packed light brown sugar

½ cup applesauce

⅓ cup canola oil

2 large eggs

1 teaspoon vanilla extract

1 medium pear, diced

½ cup unsalted roasted pumpkin seeds, divided

1.   Preheat the oven to 350°F. Coat a 12-cup muffin tin with cooking spray and set aside.

2.   In a medium bowl, sift together the all-purpose flour, pastry flour, baking powder, baking soda, and salt.

3.   In a large bowl, whisk together the almond butter, yogurt, and milk until smooth. Add the brown sugar, applesauce, and oil, and stir until combined. Add the eggs, one at a time, and the vanilla, stirring until completely incorporated.

4.   Gently fold the dry ingredients into the wet ingredients, and stir until just blended, being careful not to overmix. Gently fold in the pear and ¼ cup of pumpkin seeds.

5.   Using a ¼-cup scoop, distribute the batter among the prepared muffin cups. Tap the muffin tin a few times on the counter to release any air bubbles. Sprinkle each muffin cup with 1 teaspoon of pumpkin seeds.

6.   Bake for about 22 minutes until the tops are browned and a toothpick inserted into the center of a muffin comes out clean.

7.   Remove from the oven, and allow to cool for about 10 minutes before removing the muffins from the tin.

Storage: Place in an airtight container and keep at room temperature for 5 days. To freeze, place in a freezer-safe container or freezer bag for up to 2 months. Defrost at room temperature. Enjoy at room temperature or toast in a toaster oven.

Per Serving (1 muffin): Calories: 296; Total Fat: 15g; Saturated Fat: 2g; Protein: 9g; Total Carbs: 33g; Fiber: 3g; Sugar: 13g; Sodium: 106mg

PUMPKIN BREAKFAST BLONDIES

MAKES 15 BLONDIES

PREP TIME: 20 minutes   **COOK TIME:** 20 minutes

Who says blondies are only for dessert? This breakfast delight is made with rolled oats and pumpkin purée, making them delicious and packed with nutrition. You'll find a lot of extra flavor, using my combo of very low-calorie spices.

Nonstick cooking spray

1¼ cups whole-wheat flour or white whole-wheat flour

1½ cups rolled oats

1 teaspoon ground cinnamon

½ teaspoon baking soda

¼ teaspoon salt

¼ teaspoon ground ginger

¼ teaspoon ground allspice

⅛ teaspoon ground cloves

⅛ teaspoon ground nutmeg

2 tablespoons unsalted butter, melted

¼ cup nonfat plain Greek yogurt

½ cup 100% pure maple syrup

¼ cup light brown sugar

½ cup pumpkin purée

1 large egg

1 teaspoon vanilla extract

1. Preheat the oven to 350°F. Coat an 8-by-11.5-inch or similar size baking pan with cooking spray.

2. In a medium bowl, sift together the flour, oats, cinnamon, baking soda, salt, ginger, allspice, cloves, and nutmeg.

3. In a large bowl, whisk together the butter, yogurt, maple syrup, and brown sugar. Add the pumpkin purée, egg, and vanilla, whisking until smooth.

4. Gently fold the dry ingredients into the wet ingredients until thoroughly blended.

5. Pour the batter into the prepared pan, and use a spatula to evenly distribute. Bake for about 20 minutes until golden brown and a toothpick inserted in the center comes out clean.

6. Remove from the oven and allow the blondies to cool for 10 minutes before slicing into 15 bars.

7. Wrap each bar in plastic wrap or place in a resealable container.

Storage: Store at room temperature for up to 1 week. To freeze, place in a freezer-safe container or bag in the freezer for up to 2 months. Defrost at room temperature. Eat at room temperature or warm in a toaster oven.

TOBY'S TIP: If desired, substitute 2 teaspoons pumpkin spice blend for the cinnamon, ginger, allspice, cloves, and nutmeg.

Per Serving (1 bar): Calories: 125; Total Fat: 3g; Saturated Fat: 1g; Protein: 3g; Total Carbs: 23g; Fiber: 2g; Sugar: 10g; Sodium: 88mg

BLUEBERRY-ZUCCHINI WAFFLES

MAKES 4 WAFFLES

PREP TIME: 15 minutes   COOK TIME: 25 minutes

Zucchini can easily be incorporated into baked goods. One medium zucchini provides about 30 calories, 2 grams of fiber, and lots of vitamins C and B6. It's also a good source of vitamin K, riboflavin, folate, potassium, and manganese.

Nonstick cooking spray

1 cup unbleached all-purpose flour

1 cup whole-wheat pastry flour

2 teaspoons baking powder

1 teaspoon ground cinnamon

½ teaspoon salt

2 large eggs, beaten

¾ cup low-fat (1%) milk

¼ cup 100% pure maple syrup

½ cup unsweetened applesauce

2 tablespoons canola oil

1 medium zucchini, shredded

1 cup fresh or thawed frozen blueberries

1. Preheat a standard waffle iron and coat with cooking spray.

2. In a medium bowl, sift together the all-purpose flour, whole-wheat pastry flour, baking powder, cinnamon, and salt.

3. In a separate medium bowl, whisk together the eggs, milk, maple syrup, applesauce, and oil.

4. Gently fold the dry ingredients into the wet ingredients until just combined, being careful to not overmix. Gently fold in the zucchini and blueberries until incorporated.

5. Cook the waffles for about 6 minutes, or according to your waffle iron's instructions, using 1 cup of batter per waffle. Transfer the cooked waffle to a plate, and repeat with the remaining batter to make a total of 4 waffles.

6. Slice each waffle in half, and place one half in each of 8 resealable containers.

Storage: Place airtight containers in the refrigerator for up to 1 week. To freeze, place freezer-safe containers in the freezer for up to 2 months. To defrost, refrigerate overnight. To reheat, microwave uncovered on high for 45 seconds, or reheat in a toaster oven.

TOBY'S TIP: Top the waffles with Cranberry-Pistachio Granola with Yogurt (page 100) or the berry mixture from the Quinoa and Berries Breakfast Bowl (page 101).

Per Serving (½ waffle): Calories: 281; Total Fat: 7g; Saturated Fat: 1g; Protein: 8g; Total Carbs: 47g; Fiber: 3g; Sugar: 16g; Sodium: 359mg

CRANBERRY-PISTACHIO GRANOLA WITH YOGURT

MAKES 5 SERVINGS (WITH LEFTOVER GRANOLA)

PREP TIME: 10 minutes   COOK TIME: 30 minutes

It's tough to sort through store-bought granola and find a brand that isn't brimming with added sugar. You can save time and control ingredients by making your own batch. My version uses shelled pistachios with tart cranberries and a touch of natural sweetness from honey. This granola recipe generates about 3½ cups in total.

2 cups gluten-free rolled oats

½ cup unsalted shelled pistachios

½ cup dried cranberries

¼ teaspoon salt

½ cup honey

½ cup water, at room temperature

2½ cups nonfat plain Greek yogurt

1. Preheat the oven to 350°F. Line a sheet pan with parchment paper.

2. In a medium bowl, mix together the oats, pistachios, and cranberries. Sprinkle in the salt and stir to evenly distribute.

3. In a small bowl, whisk together the honey and water. Pour over the oat mixture and fold together to evenly coat. Allow to sit for 5 minutes to absorb the liquid.

4. Spread the oat mixture evenly on the prepared sheet pan in a thin layer. Bake, stirring every 10 minutes, until the granola is golden brown, about 30 minutes. Remove from the oven and let cool for 15 minutes.

5. Into each of 5 glass jars or containers, spoon ½ cup of yogurt and top with ¼ cup of granola.

Storage: Store covered jars in the refrigerator for up to 5 days. Extra granola can be stored in an airtight container in the pantry for up to 2 weeks.

TOBY'S TIP: There are over 300 varieties of honey available throughout the United States. Head to your local farmers' market to give some a try. The deeper-colored varieties usually have more robust flavors, while lighter-colored honey is milder.

Per Serving (1 jar): Calories: 184; Total Fat: 3g; Saturated Fat: 1g; Protein: 14g; Total Carbs: 26g; Fiber: 2g; Sugar: 17g; Sodium: 84mg
Per Serving (¼ cup granola only): Calories: 117; Total Fat: 3g; Saturated Fat: 0g; Protein: 2g; Total Carbs: 22g; Fiber: 2g; Sugar: 13g; Sodium: 43mg

QUINOA AND BERRIES BREAKFAST BOWL

MAKES 5 BOWLS

PREP TIME: 15 minutes   COOK TIME: 15 minutes

Although quinoa (a complete protein!) is commonly eaten as a savory side dish, it can also be enjoyed as a sweet hot breakfast cereal. Instead of cooking it in water or broth, this recipe cooks it in milk, which ups the protein of the dish even more.

1¼ cups quinoa

2½ cups low-fat (1%) milk

¼ cup 100% orange juice

1 tablespoon 100% pure maple syrup

½ teaspoon vanilla extract

¼ teaspoon ground cinnamon

1¼ cups fresh or thawed frozen blueberries

1¼ cups fresh strawberries, sliced

1. In a medium saucepan, bring the quinoa and milk to a boil over high heat. Reduce the heat to low, cover, and simmer until all the liquid has been absorbed, 12 to 15 minutes. Remove from the heat and fluff the quinoa with a fork.

2. In a medium bowl, whisk together the orange juice, maple syrup, vanilla, and cinnamon. Add the blueberries and strawberries, and toss to evenly coat.

3. Into each of 5 glass jars or containers, place ¾ cup of quinoa and top with ⅓ cup of berry mixture. Drizzle any extra sauce evenly into each jar.

Storage: Store covered jars in the refrigerator for up to 5 days. Quinoa can be eaten cold or at room temperature.

TOBY'S TIP: You can find quinoa in bulk at popular warehouse stores throughout the country.

Per Serving (1 jar): Calories: 257; Total Fat: 4g; Saturated Fat: 1g; Protein: 11g; Total Carbs: 45g; Fiber: 5g; Sugar: 15g; Sodium: 57mg

TROPICAL PARFAIT

MAKES 5 PARFAITS

PREP TIME: 15 minutes   **COOK TIME:** 20 minutes

Parfaits are a perfect way to combine numerous food groups: dairy, fruit, and protein. This version uses warm compote, which complements the tart flavor of the Greek yogurt.

½ cup plus 2 tablespoons unsweetened coconut flakes, divided

½ cup raw unsalted cashews, chopped

¼ cup 100% orange juice

¼ cup 100% pure maple syrup

½ teaspoon vanilla extract

½ teaspoon ground cinnamon

2 cups fresh or frozen and thawed pineapple chunks

2 cups fresh or frozen and thawed mango chunks

3¾ cups nonfat plain Greek yogurt

1.   In a large saucepan over medium-low heat, toast the coconut flakes until fragrant and slightly browned, about 3 minutes. Transfer the coconut flakes to a medium bowl and set aside to slightly cool. Use a paper towel to wipe out the saucepan.

2.   In the same saucepan over medium-low heat, toast the cashews until fragrant and slightly browned, about 4 minutes. Transfer the cashews to a small dish and set aside to slightly cool. Use a paper towel to wipe out the saucepan.

3.   In a large bowl, whisk together the orange juice, maple syrup, vanilla, and cinnamon. Add the pineapple and mango, and toss to evenly coat.

4.   Put the pineapple-mango mixture into the saucepan and bring to a boil. Reduce the heat and simmer until the pineapple and mango soften and the liquid is reduced by about half, about 10 minutes. Remove the saucepan from the heat and set aside to cool.

5.   Add the yogurt to the bowl with the toasted coconut, and toss to evenly distribute.

6.   To make the parfaits, into each of 5 glass jars, spoon ¾ cup of yogurt, top with ⅔ cup of fruit mixture (with the juices), and sprinkle with 1½ tablespoons of toasted cashews.

Storage: Store covered jars in the refrigerator for up to 5 days. Enjoy cold.

TOBY'S TIP: Swap the cashews for 1 serving of Cranberry-Pistachio Granola with Yogurt (page 100).

Per Serving (1 parfait): Calories: 351; Total Fat: 12g; Saturated Fat: 6g; Protein: 21g; Total Carbs: 43g; Fiber: 3g; Sugar: 34g; Sodium: 69mg

MAKE-AHEAD COTTAGE CHEESE AND FRUIT BOWL

MAKES 5 BOWLS

PREP TIME: 15 minutes

Although very nutritious, cottage cheese is one of the most underappreciated foods. A half-cup of low-fat cottage cheese contains 90 calories, 1 gram of fat, and 16 grams of protein. That's as much protein as in two ounces of cooked chicken! Cottage cheese is also a lactose-intolerant-friendly dairy food, with one-third the amount of lactose of 1 cup of milk.

2½ cups low-fat cottage cheese

1¼ cups seedless green or red grapes, halved

2½ cups diced cantaloupe

5 tablespoons unsalted sunflower seeds

Into each of 5 containers or glass jars, spoon ½ cup of cottage cheese. Top with ¼ cup of seedless grapes, ½ cup of cantaloupe, and 1 tablespoon of sunflower seeds.

Storage: Place airtight containers in the refrigerator for up to 5 days.

TOBY'S TIP: Instead of this recipe, try a savory spin on your cottage cheese with avocado chunks, sliced tomato, salt, and black pepper with a drizzle of balsamic vinegar.

Per Serving (1 container): Calories: 170; Total Fat: 5g; Saturated Fat: 1g; Protein: 16g; Total Carbs: 15g; Fiber: 2g; Sugar: 13g; Sodium: 472mg

PEANUT BUTTER–BANANA OATMEAL

MAKES 5 SERVINGS

PREP TIME: 10 minutes   **COOK TIME:** 5 minutes

What's better than the taste of the classic combo of peanut butter and bananas? The nutrition that these superfoods provide. Peanut butter is filled with healthy unsaturated fat, protein, niacin, and antioxidants like vitamin E and resveratrol. Bananas complement the peanut butter with fiber, vitamin B_6, vitamin C, and potassium. It's truly a match made in heaven!

2½ cups gluten-free
 quick-cooking oats

2½ cups skim milk

2½ cups water

3 tablespoons smooth
 peanut butter

3 tablespoons 100% pure
 maple syrup

1 teaspoon ground cinnamon

½ teaspoon vanilla extract

2 medium bananas,
 thinly sliced

1.   In a saucepan over medium-low heat, combine the oats, milk, and water. Bring to a simmer, stirring frequently. Cook until the oats begin to soften and the liquid thickens, about 5 minutes. Remove the pan from the heat.

2.   Stir in the peanut butter, maple syrup, cinnamon, and vanilla until evenly distributed.

3.   Divide the sliced bananas among 5 containers. Top each with 1 cup of cooled oatmeal.

Storage: Place airtight containers in the refrigerator for up to 5 days. To reheat, microwave uncovered on high for 1 minute. Stir before eating and add a splash of milk, if desired.

TOBY'S TIP: What's the difference between quick cooking and rolled oats? Quick cooking are precooked, dried, and then rolled and pressed slightly thinner than rolled oats. They cook more quickly but retain less of their texture. Old-fashioned or rolled oats absorb more liquid and hold their shape relatively well during cooking. They're commonly used in baked goods like granola bars, cookies, and muffins.

Per Serving (1 container): Calories: 333; Total Fat: 8g; Saturated Fat: 2g; Protein: 12g; Total Carbs: 55g; Fiber: 6g; Sugar: 15g; Sodium: 124mg

BANANA-STRAWBERRY OATMEAL CUPS

MAKES 12 OATMEAL CUPS

PREP TIME: 15 minutes   COOK TIME: 50 minutes

With most folks getting less than half the recommended amount of fiber each day, breakfast is the perfect opportunity to take it in. To make your morning fiber easy to grab and go, oatmeal is baked into these easily portable cups.

Nonstick cooking spray

3 cups gluten-free old-fashioned oats

1 teaspoon baking powder

1 teaspoon ground cinnamon

½ teaspoon salt

2 large eggs, beaten

1½ cups low-fat (1%) milk

1 medium banana, mashed

¼ cup 100% pure maple syrup

2 tablespoons unsalted butter, melted

1 teaspoon vanilla extract

1 cup sliced strawberries (about 8 medium)

1. Preheat the oven to 350°F. Line a 12-cup muffin tin and coat with cooking spray.

2. In a medium bowl, mix together the oats, baking powder, cinnamon, and salt.

3. In a large bowl, whisk together the eggs, milk, banana, maple syrup, butter, and vanilla.

4. Mix the dry ingredients into the wet ingredients until well combined. Fold in the sliced strawberries until evenly distributed.

5. Using a ¼-cup scoop, distribute the batter among the 12 muffin cups. Tap the muffin tin a few times on the countertop to release any air bubbles.

6. Bake for 45 to 50 minutes until the edges of the oatmeal cups are slightly browned and a toothpick inserted into the center of 1 or 2 cups comes out clean.

7. Remove from the oven and set aside to cool for 15 minutes, then transfer to a wire rack to continue cooling.

8. Place the cooled muffins in a resealable container.

Storage: Keep in an airtight container at room temperature for up to 5 days. To freeze, wrap individually or place in a freezer-safe container in the freezer for up to 2 months. Defrost at room temperature. Enjoy at room temperature or toast in a toaster oven before eating.

Per Serving (2 oatmeal cups): Calories: 298; Total Fat: 9g; Saturated Fat: 4g; Protein: 10g; Total Carbs: 46g; Fiber: 5g; Sugar: 17g; Sodium: 310mg

TRIPLE BERRY OATMEAL-ALMOND BAKE

MAKES 8 SERVINGS

PREP TIME: 15 minutes   COOK TIME: 1 hour

Berries contain powerful anti-inflammatory antioxidants that have been shown to help protect against diabetes, bolster eyesight, and lower the risk of certain types of cancer.

Nonstick cooking spray

1¾ cups gluten-free old-fashioned rolled oats

¼ cup almonds, chopped

2 teaspoons baking powder

1 teaspoon ground cinnamon

½ teaspoon salt

1½ cups low-fat (1%) milk

½ cup honey

1 large egg, beaten

1 teaspoon vanilla extract

⅔ cup fresh or thawed frozen blueberries

⅔ cup fresh or thawed frozen blackberries

⅔ cup fresh or thawed frozen raspberries

1.   Preheat the oven to 350°F. Coat an 8-by-11.5-inch baking dish with cooking spray.

2.   In a medium bowl, mix together the oats, almonds, baking powder, cinnamon, and salt.

3.   In a separate medium bowl, whisk together the milk, honey, egg, and vanilla.

4.   Pour the dry ingredients into the wet ingredients, and gently stir until just combined. Gently fold in the berries until evenly distributed.

5.   Pour the mixture into the prepared baking dish. Use a spatula or back of a spoon to evenly distribute the batter. Bake for about 1 hour until slightly browned and a toothpick inserted into the center comes out clean.

6.   Remove from the oven and allow to cool for 15 minutes before cutting into 8 even slices.

7.   Place the individual portions into 8 resealable containers.

Storage: Place airtight containers in the refrigerator for up to 1 week. To freeze, place freezer-safe containers in the freezer for up to 2 months. To defrost, refrigerate overnight. To reheat, microwave uncovered on high for 30 seconds, or warm in a toaster oven.

TOBY'S TIP: Instead of purchasing separate berries, use 2 cups of thawed frozen mixed berries.

Per Serving (1 container): Calories: 203; Total Fat: 5g; Saturated Fat: 1g; Protein: 6g; Total Carbs: 37g; Fiber: 4g; Sugar: 23g; Sodium: 268mg

VEGGIE DELIGHT BREAKFAST EGG CASSEROLE

MAKES 6 SERVINGS

PREP TIME: 20 minutes   COOK TIME: 1 hour

Eggs provide a phytonutrient called lutein, which has been shown to help keep eyesight strong. It also helps maintain the skin's elasticity and hydration and has been linked to preventing plaque buildup in your arteries.

Nonstick cooking spray

½ cup low-fat cottage cheese

8 large eggs

8 large egg whites

1 teaspoon Sriracha

½ teaspoon salt

¼ teaspoon freshly ground black pepper

½ cup shredded part-skim mozzarella cheese

¼ cup grated Parmesan cheese

1 cup cherry tomatoes, halved

3 medium carrots, peeled and shredded

1 medium zucchini, halved lengthwise and then cut into ½-inch half moons

1½ cups broccoli florets

1.   Preheat the oven to 350°F. Coat an 8-by-11.5-inch baking dish with cooking spray.

2.   In a blender, combine the cottage cheese, eggs, egg whites, Sriracha, salt, and pepper. Blend for 30 seconds to combine. Pour the egg mixture into a large bowl.

3.   Add the mozzarella and Parmesan to the egg mixture, and stir to incorporate. Add the tomatoes, carrots, zucchini, and broccoli, and toss to combine.

4.   Pour the mixture into the prepared baking dish and bake, uncovered, for 55 minutes to 1 hour until the egg mixture is set and a toothpick inserted into the center of the casserole comes out clean.

5.   Remove the casserole from the oven and allow to cool for 15 minutes before slicing into 6 pieces. Into each of 6 resealable containers, place a slice of casserole.

Storage: Place airtight containers in the refrigerator for up to 1 week. To freeze, place freezer-safe containers in the freezer for up to 2 months. Defrost in the refrigerator overnight. To reheat, microwave uncovered on high for 1½ to 2 minutes.

TOBY'S TIP: This is the perfect dish to use up leftover veggies like spinach, kale, cauliflower, pepper, sun-dried tomatoes—really, whatever you have lying around!

Per Serving (1 container): Calories: 209; Total Fat: 10g; Saturated Fat: 4g; Protein: 21g; Total Carbs: 8g; Fiber: 2g; Sugar: 4g; Sodium: 633mg

EGG AND SPINACH STUFFED PEPPERS

MAKES 5 SERVINGS

PREP TIME: 15 minutes   **COOK TIME:** 1 hour 15 minutes

Most folks don't have enough time to whip up a veggie omelet for breakfast. Instead, I make these Egg and Spinach Stuffed Peppers, which I can tote to work. This way I can get a healthy boost of protein in the morning, plus start my day with a few beneficial servings of veggies.

Nonstick cooking spray

1 tablespoon olive oil

1 small onion, chopped

1 garlic clove, minced

4 ounces button mushrooms, chopped

3 ounces baby spinach (3 cups)

1 (14.5-ounce) can no-salt-added diced tomatoes

½ teaspoon salt, divided

¼ teaspoon freshly ground black pepper, divided

5 large eggs

½ cup low-fat (1%) milk

5 large red or green bell peppers

5 teaspoons grated Parmesan cheese

1. Preheat the oven to 375°F. Coat an 8-by-11.5-inch baking dish with cooking spray.

2. In a medium skillet over medium heat, heat the oil. Add the onion and garlic, and cook until the onion softens and the garlic is fragrant, about 3 minutes. Add the mushrooms and continue cooking until they soften, about 5 minutes. Add the spinach and cook until wilted, about 5 minutes. Add the diced tomatoes, ¼ teaspoon of salt, and ⅛ teaspoon of pepper and bring to a boil. Reduce the heat and simmer until the flavors combine, about 3 minutes. Remove the skillet from the heat and allow to slightly cool.

3. In a medium bowl, whisk together the eggs, milk, and remaining ¼ teaspoon of salt and ⅛ teaspoon of pepper.

4. Slice the tops off the peppers and trim the bottoms so they stand without tilting. Using a paring knife, remove the membranes and seeds from inside each pepper. Scoop ¼ cup of vegetable mixture into each of the 5 peppers, and top each with 1 teaspoon of grated Parmesan. Then evenly distribute the egg mixture among the 5 peppers.

5. Cover the peppers loosely with aluminum foil and bake for 50 minutes. Uncover and continue baking for another 10 minutes. Remove from the oven and set aside to slightly cool.

6. Into each of 5 containers, place one stuffed pepper.

Storage: Place airtight containers in the refrigerator for up to 7 days. To freeze, place freezer-safe containers in the freezer for up to 2 months. To defrost, refrigerate overnight. To reheat, microwave uncovered on high for 1½ to 2 minutes.

TOBY'S TIP: Shake things up by stuffing a russet potato. Bake the potato, scoop out the filling, then add the veggie mix, cheese, and eggs as described above. Bake, covered, until the eggs are puffy and cooked through, about 40 minutes.

Per Serving (1 pepper): Calories: 173; Total Fat: 9g; Saturated Fat: 3g; Protein: 11g; Total Carbs: 14g; Fiber: 4g; Sugar: 8g; Sodium: 377mg

LUNCH & DINNER

≪ Sheet Pan Lemon Chicken with Potatoes and Carrots (page 126)

SWEET POTATO, KALE, AND WHITE BEAN STEW

MAKES 4 SERVINGS

PREP TIME: 15 minutes   COOK TIME: 25 minutes

One of the toughest things to plan with vegetarian or vegan meals is making sure the dish is balanced. This stew delivers, providing carbs, fiber, protein, vitamins, and minerals.

1 (15-ounce) can low-sodium cannellini beans, rinsed and drained, divided

1 tablespoon olive oil

1 medium onion, chopped

2 garlic cloves, minced

2 celery stalks, chopped

3 medium carrots, chopped

2 cups low-sodium vegetable broth

1 teaspoon apple cider vinegar

2 medium sweet potatoes, washed, peeled, and cut into bite-size chunks (about 1¼ pounds)

2 cups chopped kale

1 cup shelled edamame

¼ cup quinoa

1 teaspoon dried thyme

½ teaspoon cayenne pepper

½ teaspoon salt

¼ teaspoon freshly ground black pepper

1. Put half the beans into a blender and blend until smooth. Set aside.

2. In a large soup pot over medium heat, heat the olive oil. When the oil is shimmering, add the onion and garlic, and cook until the onion softens and the garlic is fragrant, about 3 minutes. Add the celery and carrots, and continue cooking until the vegetables soften, about 5 minutes.

3. Add the broth, vinegar, sweet potatoes, unblended beans, kale, edamame, and quinoa, and bring the mixture to a boil. Reduce the heat and simmer until the vegetables soften, about 10 minutes.

4. Add the blended beans, thyme, cayenne, salt, and black pepper, increase the heat to medium–high, and bring the mixture to a boil. Reduce the heat and simmer, uncovered, until the flavors combine, about 5 minutes.

5. Into each of 4 containers, scoop 1¾ cups of stew.

Storage: Place airtight containers in the refrigerator for up to 1 week. To freeze, place freezer-safe containers in the freezer for up to 2 months. To defrost, refrigerate overnight. To reheat individual servings, microwave uncovered on high for 2 to 2½ minutes. Alternatively, reheat the entire batch in a saucepan on the stovetop. Bring the mixture to a boil and then simmer until heated through, 10 to 15 minutes.

Per Serving (1 container): Calories: 373; Total Fat: 7g; Saturated Fat: 1g; Protein: 15g; Total Carbs: 65g; Fiber: 15g; Sugar: 13g; Sodium: 540mg

SLOW COOKER TWO-BEAN SLOPPY JOES

MAKES 4 SERVINGS

PREP TIME: 10 minutes   COOK TIME: 6 hours

Beans are hearty enough to go into the slow cooker and provide a wonderful nutrient profile that can be a vital part of a healthy eating plan. Specifically, beans are an excellent source of fiber, which most folks don't get enough of. A half-cup serving of beans provides about 7½ grams of fiber, which helps you feel fuller faster and longer, and prevents you from overeating. Studies have also found that fiber helps with cholesterol and keeps your digestive system healthy.

1 (15-ounce) can low-sodium black beans

1 (15-ounce) can low-sodium pinto beans

1 (14.5-ounce) can no-salt-added diced tomatoes

1 medium green bell pepper, cored, seeded, and chopped

1 medium yellow onion, chopped

¼ cup low-sodium vegetable broth

2 garlic cloves, minced

2 servings (¼ cup) Meal Prep Barbecue Sauce (page 90) or bottled barbecue sauce

¼ teaspoon salt

¼ teaspoon freshly ground black pepper

4 whole-wheat buns

1.   In a slow cooker, combine the black beans, pinto beans, diced tomatoes, bell pepper, onion, broth, garlic, Meal Prep Barbecue Sauce, salt, and black pepper. Stir the ingredients, then cover and cook on low for 6 hours.

2.   Into each of 4 containers, spoon 1¼ cups of sloppy Sloppy Joe mix. Serve with 1 whole-wheat bun.

Storage: Place airtight containers in the refrigerator for up to 1 week. To freeze, place freezer-safe containers in the freezer for up to 2 months. To defrost, refrigerate overnight. To reheat individual portions, microwave uncovered on high for 2 to 2½ minutes. Alternatively, reheat the entire dish in a saucepan on the stove top. Bring the Sloppy Joes to a boil, then reduce the heat and simmer until heated through, 10 to 15 minutes. Serve with a whole-wheat bun.

TOBY'S TIP: Dress up your Sloppy Joes by topping them with reduced-fat shredded Cheddar cheese, lettuce, tomato, and pickles on the side.

Per Serving (1 container plus 1 whole-wheat bun): Calories: 392; Total Fat: 3g; Saturated Fat: 0g; Protein: 17g; Total Carbs: 79g; Fiber: 19g; Sugar: 15g; Sodium: 759mg

LIGHTER EGGPLANT PARMESAN

MAKES 4 SERVINGS

PREP TIME: 15 minutes   **COOK TIME:** 35 minutes

Eating healthy doesn't mean you can't enjoy your favorite foods, like eggplant parm. In this lighter version, the eggplant is breaded in panko and baked, so you'll still get a nice crunch in every bite. It's also covered with just enough cheese without going overboard on calories and saturated fat.

Nonstick cooking spray

3 eggs, beaten

1 tablespoon dried parsley

2 teaspoons ground oregano

⅛ teaspoon freshly ground black pepper

1 cup panko bread crumbs, preferably whole-wheat

1 large eggplant (about 2 pounds)

5 servings (2½ cups) Chunky Tomato Sauce (page 89) or jarred low-sodium tomato sauce

1 cup part-skim mozzarella cheese

¼ cup grated Parmesan cheese

1. Preheat the oven to 450°F. Coat a baking sheet with cooking spray.

2. In a medium bowl, whisk together the eggs, parsley, oregano, and pepper.

3. Pour the panko into a separate medium bowl.

4. Slice the eggplant into ¼-inch-thick slices. Dip each slice of eggplant into the egg mixture, shaking off the excess. Then dredge both sides of the eggplant in the panko bread crumbs. Place the coated eggplant on the prepared baking sheet, leaving a ½-inch space between each slice.

5. Bake for about 15 minutes until soft and golden brown. Remove from the oven and set aside to slightly cool.

6. Pour ½ cup of Chunky Tomato Sauce on the bottom of an 8-by-11.5-inch baking dish. Using a spatula or the back of a spoon, spread the tomato sauce evenly. Place half the slices of cooked eggplant, slightly overlapping, in the dish, and top with 1 cup of Chunky Tomato Sauce, ½ cup of mozzarella and 2 tablespoons of grated Parmesan. Repeat the layer, ending with the cheese.

7. Bake uncovered for 20 minutes until the cheese is bubbling and slightly browned.

8. Remove from the oven and allow to cool for 15 minutes before dividing the eggplant equally into 4 separate containers.

Storage: Place airtight containers in the refrigerator for up to 1 week. To freeze, place freezer-safe containers in the freezer for up to 2 months. To defrost, refrigerate overnight. To reheat individual portions, microwave uncovered on high for 2 to 2½ minutes. Alternatively, reheat the entire dish in a 350°F oven until warmed through, about 15 minutes.

> **TOBY'S TIP:** This dish pairs nicely with Roasted Broccoli with Shallots (page 148).

Per Serving (1 container): Calories: 333; Total Fat: 14g; Saturated Fat: 6g; Protein: 20g; Total Carbs: 35g; Fiber: 11g; Sugar: 15g; Sodium: 994mg

COCONUT-LENTIL CURRY

MAKES 4 SERVINGS

PREP TIME: 15 minutes   **COOK TIME:** 35 minutes

Lentils are nutritional superstars because they provide healthy protein and complex carbohydrates, and they're full of fiber to keep you satisfied longer. The soluble fiber found has also been shown to help lower cholesterol. One cup of cooked lentils provides 230 calories, 37 percent of your daily recommended amount of iron, and more than half your daily fiber. These babies are also known to be heart healthy.

1 tablespoon olive oil

1 medium yellow onion, chopped

1 garlic clove, minced

1 medium red bell pepper, diced

1 (15-ounce) can green or brown lentils, rinsed and drained

2 medium sweet potatoes, washed, peeled, and cut into bite-size chunks (about 1¼ pounds)

1 (14.5-ounce) can no-salt-added diced tomatoes

2 tablespoons tomato paste

4 teaspoons curry powder

⅛ teaspoon ground cloves

1 (13.5-ounce) can light coconut milk

¼ teaspoon salt

2 pieces whole-wheat naan bread, halved, or 4 slices crusty bread

1. In a large saucepan over medium heat, heat the olive oil. When the oil is shimmering, add the onion and garlic and cook until the onion softens and the garlic is fragrant, about 3 minutes.

2. Add the bell pepper and continue cooking until it softens, about 5 minutes more. Add the lentils, sweet potatoes, tomatoes, tomato paste, curry powder, and cloves, and bring the mixture to a boil. Reduce the heat to medium-low, cover, and simmer until the potatoes are softened, about 20 minutes.

3. Add the coconut milk and salt, and return to a boil. Reduce the heat and simmer until the flavors combine, about 5 minutes.

4. Into each of 4 containers, spoon 2 cups of curry.

5. Enjoy each serving with half of a piece of naan bread or 1 slice of crusty bread.

Storage: Place airtight containers (without the bread) in the refrigerator for up to 1 week. To freeze, place freezer-safe containers in the freezer for up to 2 months. To defrost, refrigerate overnight. To reheat individual portions, microwave uncovered on high for 2 to 2½ minutes. Alternatively, reheat the entire curry in a saucepan on the stove top. Bring the curry to a boil, then reduce the heat and simmer until heated through, 10 to 15 minutes. Serve with the bread.

TOBY'S TIP: For variation, swap the bell pepper for 2 chopped carrots.

Per Serving (1 container): Calories: 559; Total Fat: 16g; Saturated Fat: 7g; Protein: 16g; Total Carbs: 86g; Fiber: 16g; Sugar: 18g; Sodium: 819mg

STUFFED PORTOBELLO WITH CHEESE

MAKES 4 SERVINGS

PREP TIME: 15 minutes   COOK TIME: 25 minutes

Portobello mushrooms have a meaty texture and are packed with nutrients like fiber, B vitamins, copper, and potassium. Mushrooms are also a source of the antioxidant selenium, which helps strengthen the immune system and also protects body cells from damage.

4 portobello mushroom caps

1 tablespoon olive oil

½ teaspoon salt, divided

¼ teaspoon freshly ground black pepper, divided

1 cup baby spinach, chopped

1½ cups part-skim ricotta cheese

½ cup part-skim shredded mozzarella cheese

¼ cup grated Parmesan cheese

1 garlic clove, minced

1 tablespoon dried parsley

2 teaspoons dried oregano

4 teaspoons unseasoned bread crumbs, divided

4 servings (4 cups) Roasted Broccoli with Shallots (page 148)

1.   Preheat the oven to 375°F. Line a baking sheet with aluminum foil.

2.   Brush the mushroom caps with the olive oil, and sprinkle with ¼ teaspoon salt and ⅛ teaspoon pepper. Put the mushroom caps on the prepared baking sheet and bake until soft, about 12 minutes.

3.   In a medium bowl, mix together the spinach, ricotta, mozzarella, Parmesan, garlic, parsley, oregano, and the remaining ¼ teaspoon of salt and ⅛ teaspoon of pepper.

4.   Spoon ½ cup of cheese mixture into each mushroom cap, and sprinkle each with 1 teaspoon of bread crumbs. Return the mushrooms to the oven for an additional 8 to 10 minutes until warmed through.

5.   Remove from the oven and allow the mushrooms to cool for about 10 minutes before placing each in an individual container. Add 1 cup of Roasted Broccoli with Shallots to each container.

Storage: Place airtight containers in the refrigerator for up to 1 week. To reheat, microwave uncovered on high for 2 to 2½ minutes.

TOBY'S TIP: To make this dish gluten-free, either use gluten-free bread crumbs or omit the bread crumbs.

Per Serving (1 container): Calories: 419; Total Fat: 30g; Saturated Fat: 10g; Protein: 23g; Total Carbs: 19g; Fiber: 2g; Sugar: 3g; Sodium: 790mg

LIGHTER SHRIMP SCAMPI

MAKES 4 SERVINGS

PREP TIME: 15 minutes   **COOK TIME:** 15 minutes

In my first cookbook, *The Greek Yogurt Kitchen*, I lightened a hollandaise sauce that is traditionally made with a boatload of butter. The results were so good that I landed an interview on *The Dr. Oz Show*, where I showed millions how to whip it up. This scampi dish is no different. Instead of a half-stick of butter, I use just 2 tablespoons in the sauce, and the flavor is still unbelievable.

1½ pounds large peeled and deveined shrimp

¼ teaspoon salt

⅛ teaspoon freshly ground black pepper

2 tablespoons olive oil

1 shallot, chopped

2 garlic cloves, minced

¼ cup cooking white wine

Juice of ½ lemon (1 tablespoon)

½ teaspoon Sriracha

2 tablespoons unsalted butter, at room temperature

¼ cup chopped fresh parsley

4 servings (6 cups) Zucchini Noodles with Lemon Vinaigrette (page 146)

1. Season the shrimp with the salt and pepper.

2. In a medium saucepan over medium heat, heat the oil. Add the shallot and garlic, and cook until the shallot softens and the garlic is fragrant, about 3 minutes. Add the shrimp, cover, and cook until opaque, 2 to 3 minutes on each side. Using a slotted spoon, transfer the shrimp to a large plate.

3. Add the wine, lemon juice, and Sriracha to the saucepan, and stir to combine. Bring the mixture to a boil, then reduce the heat and simmer until the liquid is reduced by about half, 3 minutes. Add the butter and stir until melted, about 3 minutes. Return the shrimp to the saucepan and toss to coat. Add the parsley and stir to combine.

4. Into each of 4 containers, place 1½ cups of Zucchini Noodles with Lemon Vinaigrette, and top with ¾ cup of scampi.

Storage: Place airtight containers in the refrigerator for up to 3 days. To reheat, microwave uncovered on high for about 2 minutes.

TOBY'S TIP: Serve the shrimp scampi over whole-grain pasta or plain, unflavored zucchini noodles.

Per Serving (1 container): Calories: 364; Total Fat: 21g; Saturated Fat: 6g; Protein: 37g; Total Carbs: 10g; Fiber: 2g; Sugar: 6g; Sodium: 557mg

MAPLE-MUSTARD SALMON

MAKES 4 SERVINGS

PREP TIME: 10 minutes, plus 30 minutes marinating time   COOK TIME: 20 minutes

The American Heart Association recommends at least two 3½-ounce servings of fatty fish per week. Omega-3 fats have shown heart health benefits including decreasing the risk of abnormal heartbeats and slowing down the rate of plaque buildup. This simple salmon dish is a quick yet delicious way to take in your omega-3s.

Nonstick cooking spray

½ cup 100% maple syrup

2 tablespoons Dijon mustard

¼ teaspoon salt

4 (5-ounce) salmon fillets

4 servings (4 cups) Roasted Broccoli with Shallots (page 148)

4 servings (2 cups) Parsleyed Whole-Wheat Couscous (page 144)

1.   Preheat the oven to 400°F. Line a baking sheet with aluminum foil and coat with cooking spray.

2.   In a medium bowl, whisk together the maple syrup, mustard, and salt until smooth.

3.   Put the salmon fillets into the bowl and toss to coat. Cover and place in the refrigerator to marinate for at least 30 minutes and up to overnight.

4.   Shake off excess marinade from the salmon fillets and place them on the prepared baking sheet, leaving a 1-inch space between each fillet. Discard the extra marinade.

5.   Bake for about 20 minutes until the salmon is opaque and a thermometer inserted in the thickest part of a fillet reads 145°F.

6.   Into each of 4 resealable containers, place 1 salmon fillet, 1 cup of Roasted Broccoli with Shallots, and ½ cup of Parsleyed Whole-Wheat Couscous.

Storage: Place airtight containers in the refrigerator for up to 5 days. To freeze, place freezer-safe containers in the freezer for up to 2 months. To defrost, refrigerate overnight. To reheat, microwave uncovered on high for 2 to 3 minutes.

TOBY'S TIP: Swap the salmon for tuna fillets. Bake at 450°F for 15 to 20 minutes, depending on thickness.

Per Serving (1 container): Calories: 601; Total Fat: 29g; Saturated Fat: 4g; Protein: 36g; Total Carbs: 51g; Fiber: 3g; Sugar: 23g; Sodium: 610mg

LEMON-CAPER TILAPIA WITH WHOLE-WHEAT COUSCOUS

MAKES 4 SERVINGS

PREP TIME: 10 minutes   **COOK TIME:** 20 minutes

Many unnecessary calories and artery-clogging saturated fat derive from sauces that drown the food. You can still enjoy flavorful sauces, but in much smaller portions, while also being able to taste the clean flavor of the fish. In this simple recipe, just one heaping tablespoon of lemon-caper sauce provides a salty burst of flavor that your taste buds will love.

Nonstick cooking spray

4 (6-ounce) tilapia fillets

2 tablespoons olive oil, divided

¼ teaspoon salt

⅛ teaspoon freshly ground black pepper

1 garlic clove, minced

¾ cup low-sodium vegetable broth

Juice of ½ lemon (1 tablespoon)

2 tablespoons capers, with liquid

1 tablespoon unbleached all-purpose flour

2 tablespoons chopped fresh parsley

4 servings (2 cups) Parsleyed Whole-Wheat Couscous (page 144)

4 servings (4 cups) Roasted Broccoli with Shallots (page 148)

1.   Preheat the oven to 350°F. Coat a baking sheet with cooking spray.

2.   Brush the fish with 1 tablespoon of olive oil and sprinkle with the salt and pepper.

3.   Place the fish on the prepared baking sheet and bake for about 15 minutes until the fish flakes easily with a fork and reaches a minimum internal cooking temperature of 145°F.

4.   In a medium saucepan over medium heat, heat the remaining 1 tablespoon of oil. When the oil is shimmering, add the garlic and cook until fragrant, about 30 seconds. Add the vegetable broth, and use a wooden spoon to scrape any bits of garlic off the bottom of the pan. Bring the mixture to a boil, then reduce the heat to medium-low and simmer until the liquid is reduced by half, about 2 minutes.

5.   Add the lemon juice and capers, and stir to combine.

6. Sprinkle the mixture with the flour and bring to a boil. Reduce the heat to medium-low and simmer, stirring regularly, until the mixture thickens, about 2 minutes. Stir in the chopped parsley.

7. Into each of 4 containers, place 1 fish fillet and top with 1 heaping tablespoon of pan sauce. Spoon ½ cup of Parsleyed Whole-Wheat Couscous and 1 cup of Roasted Broccoli with Shallots on the side.

Storage: Place airtight containers in the refrigerator for up to 5 days. To reheat, microwave uncovered on high for 2 to 2½ minutes.

TOBY'S TIP: Swap the fish for skinless, boneless chicken breasts and cook until they reach an internal cooking temperature of 165°F.

Per Serving (1 container): Calories: 546; Total Fat: 29g; Saturated Fat: 5g; Protein: 43g; Total Carbs: 34g; Fiber: 4g; Sugar: 3g; Sodium: 684mg

BAKED "FRIED" FISH WITH CAJUN CHIPS

MAKES 4 SERVINGS

PREP TIME: 20 minutes   COOK TIME: 40 minutes

Whitefish like flounder is figure-friendly, with 100 calories, 1 gram of fat, and 21 grams of protein per 3-ounce cooked serving. It's also an excellent source of vitamin B_{12}, phosphorus, and selenium, and a good source of vitamin B_6 and magnesium. Breading and baking help keep the calories low, and adding some fiery Cajun spice to the baked fries complements the flavor of the mild fish.

FOR THE FISH

Nonstick cooking spray

2 large eggs plus 2 large egg whites

1 tablespoon onion powder

1 tablespoon garlic powder

1 tablespoon dried parsley

2 teaspoons dried oregano

¼ teaspoon salt

⅛ teaspoon freshly ground black pepper

2 cups unflavored (plain) bread crumbs

4 (5-ounce) fillets flounder, sole, or other white flaky fish

FOR THE CAJUN FRIES

2 russet potatoes, washed and cut into ½-inch thick strips (about 1½ pounds)

2 tablespoons olive oil

1 teaspoon Cajun seasoning

1.   Preheat the oven to 375°F. Coat a baking sheet with cooking spray.

2.   In a medium bowl, whisk together the eggs, egg whites, onion powder, garlic powder, parsley, oregano, salt, and pepper.

3.   Into a separate medium bowl or deep dish, pour the bread crumbs and spread them evenly.

4.   Dip 1 piece of fish in the egg mixture, then dredge in the bread crumbs. Again, dip the piece of fish in the egg mixture and then the bread crumbs, this time pressing down firmly to make sure the crumbs stick to the fish. Place the fish on the prepared baking sheet. Repeat with the remaining 3 pieces of fish.

5.   Bake until crispy and lightly browned, about 20 minutes. Remove the baking sheet from the oven and set aside to cool.

6.   To make the Cajun fries, increase the oven temperature to 400°F. Line a baking sheet with aluminum foil and coat with cooking spray.

7.   In a large bowl, combine the potatoes, oil, and Cajun seasoning. Toss to thoroughly coat the potatoes.

8. Spread the fries in a single layer on the prepared baking sheet, and bake until browned, 20 minutes.

9. Into each of 4 containers, place 1 piece of fish and about 1 cup of fries.

Storage: Place airtight containers in the refrigerator for up to 5 days. To reheat, microwave uncovered on high for 1½ to 2 minutes.

TOBY'S TIP: Swap the russets with sweet potatoes.

Per Serving (1 container): Calories: 537; Total Fat: 15g; Saturated Fat: 3g; Protein: 33g; Total Carbs: 68g; Fiber: 5g; Sugar: 4g; Sodium: 1,100mg

CHICKEN SALAD WITH GRAPES AND PECANS

PREP TIME: 15 minutes   **COOK TIME:** 5 minutes

You'll often find that I add nuts to recipes, to up not only the flavor but also the nutrition. Nuts like pecans are filled with healthy unsaturated fat and also have great health benefits. A 2011 study published in *The Journal of Nutrition* found that the antioxidant vitamin E, along with other compounds found in pecans, might play a protective role in the fight against heart disease.

⅓ cup unsalted pecans, chopped

10 ounces cooked skinless, boneless chicken breast or rotisserie chicken, finely chopped

½ medium yellow onion, finely chopped

1 celery stalk, finely chopped

¾ cup red or green seedless grapes, halved

¼ cup light mayonnaise

¼ cup nonfat plain Greek yogurt

1 tablespoon Dijon mustard

1 tablespoon dried parsley

¼ teaspoon salt

⅛ teaspoon freshly ground black pepper

1 cup shredded romaine lettuce

4 (8-inch) whole-wheat pitas

1. Heat a small skillet over medium-low heat to toast the pecans. Cook the pecans until fragrant, about 3 minutes. Remove from the heat and set aside to cool.

2. In a medium bowl, mix the chicken, onion, celery, pecans, and grapes.

3. In a small bowl, whisk together the mayonnaise, yogurt, mustard, parsley, salt, and pepper. Spoon the sauce over the chicken mixture and stir until well combined.

4. Into each of 4 containers, place ¼ cup of lettuce and top with 1 cup of chicken salad. Store the pitas separately until ready to serve.

5. When ready to eat, stuff the serving of salad and lettuce into 1 pita.

Storage: Place airtight containers in the refrigerator for up to 5 days.

TOBY'S TIP: To make this dish gluten-free, omit the pita, and pack and serve the chicken salad over a green salad with lettuce or baby spinach, tomatoes, and cucumbers.

Per Serving (1 container plus 1 pita): Calories: 418; Total Fat: 14g; Saturated Fat: 2g; Protein: 31g; Total Carbs: 43g; Fiber: 6g; Sugar: 6g; Sodium: 718mg

HEARTY CHICKEN SOUP WITH VEGETABLES AND QUINOA

MAKES 4 SERVINGS

PREP TIME: 15 minutes   COOK TIME: 25 minutes

On a cold day, there's nothing better than a warming bowl of soup. This version was created to be a quick and easy meal with protein, vegetables, and whole grains. With 34 grams of protein and 8 grams of fiber, this steaming bowl of goodness will keep you satisfied.

1 tablespoon olive oil

1 medium yellow onion, chopped

2 garlic cloves, minced

2 medium carrots, peeled and chopped

2 celery stalks, chopped

8 ounces cubed skinless leftover chicken or rotisserie chicken

7 cups low-sodium chicken broth

1 (14.5-ounce) can no-salt-added diced tomatoes

1 cup frozen peas

1 cup frozen green beans

¼ cup quinoa

2 bay leaves

1 tablespoon dried parsley

1 teaspoon dried thyme

½ teaspoon salt

¼ teaspoon freshly ground black pepper

16 whole-grain crackers

1. In a large pot over medium heat, heat the olive oil. When the oil is shimmering, add the onion, garlic, carrots, and celery, and cook until the vegetables soften, about 4 minutes.

2. Add the chicken and stir to incorporate. Add the broth, tomatoes, peas, green beans, quinoa, bay leaves, parsley, thyme, salt, and pepper, and stir. Bring the soup to a boil, then reduce the heat and simmer, partially covered, until the flavors combine and the quinoa is cooked, 20 minutes. Remove and discard the bay leaves.

3. Ladle 2½ cups of soup into each of 4 glass jars or containers. Store the crackers separately until ready to serve.

4. Serve the soup with 4 crackers on the side.

Storage: Place airtight jars in the refrigerator for up to 1 week. To freeze, place freezer-safe containers in the freezer for up to 2 months. To defrost, refrigerate overnight. To reheat individual portions, microwave uncovered on high for 2 to 2½ minutes. Alternatively, reheat the entire soup in a pot on the stove top. Bring the soup to a boil, then reduce the heat and simmer until heated through, about 10 minutes. Serve with crackers.

TOBY'S TIP: The serving size of crackers varies widely. If you're watching portions, check the label to make sure you're taking 1 serving.

Per Serving (1 container, plus 4 crackers): Calories: 400; Total Fat: 12g; Saturated Fat: 2g; Protein: 34g; Total Carbs: 43g; Fiber: 8g; Sugar: 9g; Sodium: 757mg

SHEET PAN LEMON CHICKEN WITH POTATOES AND CARROTS

MAKES 4 SERVINGS

PREP TIME: 15 minutes   COOK TIME: 45 minutes

Potatoes have a bad reputation in some circles, but they actually add quite a bit of nutrition to a meal. One medium red spud contains 154 calories, 3 grams of fiber, 36 percent of your daily vitamin C needs, 27 percent of your daily potassium needs (more than bananas!), and a slew of B vitamins. Many of these nutrients, including fiber and some iron, come from the potato skin, so feel free to keep them on.

Nonstick cooking spray

¼ cup olive oil

2 lemons, 1 juiced and 1 thinly sliced

2 tablespoons chopped fresh rosemary

2 garlic cloves, minced

½ teaspoon salt

¼ teaspoon freshly ground black pepper

1½ pounds skinless, boneless chicken thighs

1½ pounds new potatoes, quartered

5 medium carrots, cut into ½-inch coins (about 1 pound)

2 medium parsnips, cut into ½-inch coins (about ½ pound)

1. Preheat the oven to 425°F. Coat a sheet pan with cooking spray.

2. In a large bowl, whisk together the olive oil, lemon juice, rosemary, garlic, salt, and pepper.

3. Add the chicken, potatoes, carrots, and parsnips to the dressing and toss to coat.

4. Gently pour the vegetables and chicken onto the prepared baking sheet, making sure they are in a single layer. Top with the lemon slices. Place in the oven and roast for 40 to 45 minutes until the chicken reaches a minimum internal cooking temperature of 165°F.

5. Into each of 4 containers, scoop about 2 cups of chicken and vegetables.

Storage: Place airtight containers in the refrigerator for up to 1 week. To freeze, place freezer-safe containers in the freezer for up to 2 months. To defrost, refrigerate overnight. To reheat individual portions, microwave uncovered on high for 2 to 2½ minutes.

TOBY'S TIP: To minimize food waste, add leftover vegetables like carrots, beets, or Brussels sprouts to this mix.

Per Serving (1 container): Calories: 510; Total Fat: 19g; Saturated Fat: 3g; Protein: 33g; Total Carbs: 53g; Fiber: 9g; Sugar: 9g; Sodium: 596mg

SESAME CHICKEN WITH ASPARAGUS AND RED PEPPERS

MAKES 4 SERVINGS

PREP TIME: 15 minutes   COOK TIME: 20 minutes

The shape of a wok allows for the use of a small amount of oil—only about 2 tablespoons for a recipe that serves 4 people. If you love stir-frying, I recommend purchasing a carbon steel stove-top wok. If you don't have a wok, a skillet can also get the job done.

FOR THE SAUCE

¼ cup low-sodium soy sauce

⅓ cup honey

1 tablespoon unseasoned rice vinegar

1 garlic clove, minced

FOR THE STIR-FRY

2 tablespoons sesame oil or olive oil

1 pound boneless, skinless chicken breast, cut into 1-inch cubes

1 medium red pepper, cut into ½-inch strips

12 asparagus spears (about ½ bunch), trimmed and cut into thirds

1 tablespoon sesame seeds

4 servings (3 cups) Herbed Quinoa (page 140)

TO MAKE THE SAUCE

In a small bowl, whisk together the soy sauce, honey, rice vinegar, and garlic.

TO MAKE THE STIR-FRY

1.   In a large wok or skillet over medium-high heat, heat the oil. Add the chicken and cook on all sides, turning occasionally, for about 8 minutes.

2.   Add the pepper and asparagus to the wok and toss to combine. Cook until the vegetables begin to soften, about 5 minutes. Add the sauce and stir to evenly coat the chicken and vegetables. Bring the mixture to a boil, then reduce the heat to a simmer. Continue cooking for about 5 minutes until the flavors combine and a thermometer inserted into the chicken reads 165°F.

3.   Remove the wok from the heat and sprinkle with the sesame seeds.

4.   Into each of 4 containers, place 1 cup of stir-fry and ¾ cup of Herbed Quinoa.

Storage: Store covered containers in the refrigerator for up to 5 days. To reheat, microwave uncovered on high for about 2 minutes.

Per Serving (1 container): Calories: 589; Total Fat: 24g; Saturated Fat: 4g; Protein: 35g; Total Carbs: 60g; Fiber: 6g; Sugar: 28g; Sodium: 809mg

CHICKEN PAD THAI
OVER ZUCCHINI NOODLES

MAKES 4 SERVINGS

PREP TIME: 15 minutes   COOK TIME: 15 minutes

You don't have to go to a restaurant to enjoy delicious Thai food. This lighter version features a homemade pad Thai sauce, which you can use with shrimp, too.

¼ cup low-sodium chicken broth

3 tablespoons unseasoned rice vinegar

Juice of ½ lime (about 1 tablespoon)

3 tablespoons brown sugar

1½ tablespoons fish sauce

1 tablespoon low-sodium soy sauce

1¼ pounds skinless, boneless chicken breast, cut into 1-inch slices

⅛ teaspoon freshly ground black pepper

2 tablespoons olive oil

2 scallions, chopped (white and green parts)

¼ cup unsalted dry roasted peanuts, chopped

4 servings (3 cups) Zucchini Noodles with Lemon Vinaigrette (page 146)

1. In a small bowl, whisk together the broth, vinegar, lime juice, brown sugar, fish sauce, and soy sauce.

2. Sprinkle the chicken with the pepper.

3. In a medium saucepan over medium heat, heat the oil. When the oil is shimmering, add the chicken and cook on all sides, tossing occasionally, for 8 minutes. Using a slotted spoon, transfer the chicken to a large plate.

4. Add the sauce to the saucepan and bring to a boil. Reduce the heat and cook until the liquid is reduced by half, about 5 minutes. Return the chicken to the saucepan and toss to coat. Sprinkle with the scallions and peanuts.

5. Into each of 4 containers, place 1½ cups of Zucchini Noodles with Lemon Vinaigrette and top with ¾ cup of chicken. Spoon the extra sauce among the 4 containers.

Storage: Place airtight containers in the refrigerator for up to 3 days, or store the zucchini noodles separately and the pad thai can remain in the refrigerator for up to 1 week. To reheat, microwave uncovered on high for about 2 minutes.

TOBY'S TIP: Swap the zucchini noodles for soba or buckwheat noodles. Follow the package's cooking instructions.

Per Serving (1 container): Calories: 400; Total Fat: 23g; Saturated Fat: 3g; Protein: 34g; Total Carbs: 17g; Fiber: 3g; Sugar: 13g; Sodium: 1,149mg

SESAME-SOY PORK CHOPS WITH BROCCOLI AND FARRO

PREP TIME: 10 minutes, plus 30 minutes marinating time   COOK TIME: 10 minutes

Thanks to increased trimming practices, many cuts of fresh pork are leaner today compared to two decades ago. According to the National Pork Board, today's cuts on average are about 16 percent lower in total fat and 27 percent lower in saturated fat. There are seven cuts of pork, also referred to as the "Slim 7," that meet the USDA guidelines for "lean" or "extra lean," including pork tenderloin, sirloin pork chop, New York pork chop, ground pork (96 percent lean), New York pork roast, porterhouse pork chop, and rib-eye pork chop.

---

2 tablespoons low-sodium soy sauce

Juice of 1 lime (about 2 tablespoons)

2 tablespoons honey

1 teaspoon sesame oil

2 teaspoons unseasoned rice vinegar

2 garlic cloves, minced

¼ teaspoon ground ginger

4 (6-ounce) boneless pork loin chops

Nonstick cooking spray, or 1 tablespoon olive oil

4 servings (2 cups) Farro with Peas (page 141)

4 servings (4 cups) Roasted Broccoli with Shallots (page 148)

1. In a medium bowl, whisk together the soy sauce, lime juice, honey, sesame oil, rice vinegar, garlic, and ginger. Add the pork chops and toss to evenly coat. Cover and refrigerate for at least 30 minutes and up to overnight.

2. Coat a grill pan with cooking spray and heat over medium heat. Alternatively, brush the grates of an outdoor grill with the olive oil. When the pan or grill is hot, cook the pork chops for 3 to 5 minutes on each side until they reach an internal cooking temperature of 145°F.

3. Into each of 4 containers, spoon ½ cup of Farro with Peas and 1 cup of Roasted Broccoli with Shallots. Top each with 1 pork chop.

Storage: Place airtight containers in the refrigerator for up to 1 week. To freeze, place freezer-safe containers in the freezer for up to 2 months. To defrost, refrigerate overnight. To reheat, microwave uncovered on high for about 2½ minutes.

> **TOBY'S TIP:** Swap the pork for boneless, skinless chicken breast or shrimp and adjust the cooking time accordingly. Chicken may need a few more minutes while shrimp a few less.

Per Serving (1 container): Calories: 570; Total Fat: 27g; Saturated Fat: 5g; Protein: 46g; Total Carbs: 39g; Fiber: 6g; Sugar: 7g; Sodium: 643mg

SUN-DRIED TOMATO AND FETA MEATBALLS

MAKES 4 SERVINGS

PREP TIME: 15 minutes   **COOK TIME:** 20 minutes

Lean ground meats are lighter in calories but admittedly need a punch of flavor. Herbs, chopped olives, and even mushrooms can be added as go-to flavor enhancers. This recipe adds color and nutrition with sun-dried tomatoes and feta.

1 pound ground pork

1 medium yellow onion, finely chopped

1 garlic clove, minced

1 large egg, beaten

½ cup panko bread crumbs, preferably whole-wheat

¼ cup sun-dried tomatoes in oil, drained and chopped

⅓ cup crumbled feta cheese

¼ cup fresh basil leaves, chopped

¼ teaspoon salt

⅛ teaspoon freshly ground black pepper

2 tablespoons olive or canola oil

4 servings (2 cups) Chunky Tomato Sauce (page 89) or 2 cups jarred tomato sauce

4 servings (3 cups) Zucchini Noodles with Lemon Vinaigrette (page 146)

1. In a large bowl, mix together the ground pork, onion, garlic, egg, bread crumbs, sun-dried tomatoes, feta, basil, salt, and pepper.

2. Shape 1 tablespoon of pork mixture into a ball and place on a large plate. Repeat with the remaining mixture to make about 20 meatballs.

3. In a large skillet over medium heat, heat the olive oil. When the oil is shimmering, add the meatballs, cover, and cook for about 15 minutes, browning on all sides until a thermometer inserted into a meatball reads 155°F.

4. Add the Chunky Tomato Sauce and toss to evenly coat. Bring to a boil, reduce the heat to medium, and cook until the sauce is heated through.

5. Into each of 4 containers, place 1½ cups of Zucchini Noodles with Lemon Vinaigrette. Top each serving with 5 meatballs.

Storage: Place airtight containers in the refrigerator for up to 3 days, or store the zucchini noodles separately and the meatballs (with or without sauce) can remain in the refrigerator for up to 1 week. To freeze, place freezer-safe containers in the freezer for up to 2 months. To defrost, refrigerate overnight. To reheat individual portions, microwave uncovered on high for 2 to 2½ minutes. Alternatively, reheat the entire batch of meatballs with sauce in a saucepan on the stove top. Bring the sauce to a boil, then reduce the heat and simmer until heated through, 10 to 15 minutes.

Per Serving (1 container): Calories: 463; Total Fat: 27g; Saturated Fat: 6g; Protein: 33g; Total Carbs: 27g; Fiber: 5g; Sugar: 13g; Sodium: 1,125mg

SIMPLE MEAT SAUCE WITH WHOLE-WHEAT SPAGHETTI

MAKES 6 SERVINGS

PREP TIME: 15 minutes   **COOK TIME:** 55 minutes

One of the basic dishes I learned to make in my twenties is meat sauce. It freezes well, is easy to make, and is filled with good-for-you nutrients. Once you give this recipe a few rounds, you'll be an expert and make it a regular part of your healthy eating plan.

1 tablespoon olive oil

1 medium onion, chopped

1 garlic clove, minced

1 pound 90% to 92% lean ground beef

1 (28-ounce) can crushed tomatoes

1 (8-ounce) can no-salt-added tomato sauce or 1 cup Chunky Tomato Sauce (page 89)

2 tablespoons tomato paste

2 tablespoons brown sugar

1 tablespoon dried basil

1 tablespoon dried parsley

2 teaspoons dried oregano

3 bay leaves

½ teaspoon salt

¼ teaspoon freshly ground black pepper

12 ounces whole-wheat spaghetti

6 servings (6 cups) Roasted Broccoli with Shallots (page 148)

1. In a medium saucepan over medium heat, heat the olive oil. When the oil is shimmering, add the onion and garlic, and cook until the onion is translucent and garlic is fragrant, about 3 minutes.

2. Add the ground beef and use a wooden spoon to break apart the pieces. Cook until the ground beef is browned on all sides, about 8 minutes.

3. Add the crushed tomatoes, tomato sauce, tomato paste, brown sugar, basil, parsley, oregano, bay leaves, salt, and pepper, and stir to combine. Bring the mixture to a boil, then reduce the heat and simmer until the flavors combine and the beef is cooked through, about 30 minutes.

4. While the sauce is simmering, bring a large pot of water to a boil. Add the spaghetti and bring to a boil. Reduce the heat and simmer until the spaghetti is al dente, about 12 minutes. Drain the pasta and set aside to cool.

5. Remove and discard the bay leaves from the sauce. Into each of 6 containers, place 1¼ cups of spaghetti and top with ¾ cup of meat sauce. Add 1 cup of Roasted Broccoli with Shallots on top.

Storage: Place airtight containers in the refrigerator for up to 1 week. To freeze, place freezer-safe containers in the freezer for up to 2 months. To defrost, refrigerate overnight. To reheat individual portions, microwave uncovered on high for 2 to 2½ minutes. Alternatively, reheat the entire meat sauce in a saucepan on the stove top. Bring the sauce to a boil, then reduce the heat and simmer until heated through, 10 to 15 minutes.

> **TOBY'S TIP:** Replace the whole-wheat spaghetti with Cauliflower Rice with Mushrooms (page 145) or Zucchini Noodles with Lemon Vinaigrette (page 146).

Per Serving (1 container): Calories: 586; Total Fat: 25g; Saturated Fat: 6g; Protein: 30g; Total Carbs: 68g; Fiber: 5g; Sugar: 11g; Sodium: 712mg

SLOW COOKER POT ROAST WITH CARROTS AND MUSHROOMS

MAKES 6 SERVINGS

PREP TIME: 15 minutes   COOK TIME: 20 minutes, plus 4 hours on high or 8 hours on low

Pot roast isn't really a cut of meat—it's more of a cooking method. Choose a large chunk of tough beef and brown it on the stove top for a few minutes. Then place it in the slow cooker with vegetables, liquids, herbs and spices, cover, and sit back until you get a tender, delicious meal.

2 tablespoons olive oil

1 (2¾-pound) bottom round rump roast or boneless shoulder steak

2 small onions, quartered

6 carrots, peeled and cut into 1-inch coins

1 (8-ounce) container white capped mushrooms, washed and halved

½ cup red cooking wine

1¼ cups low-sodium beef or vegetable broth

2 garlic cloves, minced

½ teaspoon salt

¼ teaspoon freshly ground black pepper

3 tablespoons cornstarch

1. In a large saucepan over medium heat, heat the oil. When the oil is shimmering, add the beef and cook for 5 minutes on each side.

2. Into a slow cooker, put the beef, onions, carrots, mushrooms, wine, broth, garlic, salt, and pepper. Toss to evenly coat the beef with the liquids. Cover and cook on high for 4 hours or low for 8 hours.

3. Transfer the beef to a cutting board to cool.

4. Strain and reserve the liquid from the slow cooker, and skim off any visible fat. Spoon ¾ cup of the reserved liquid into a small bowl and whisk with the cornstarch.

5. In a medium saucepan, bring the remaining reserved liquid to a boil, then reduce the heat and simmer. Add the cornstarch slurry to the saucepan, and whisk continuously until the liquid thickens, about 10 minutes.

6. Thinly slice the roast. Into each of 6 containers, place 4 ounces of roast with ⅔ cup of vegetables and top with ⅓ cup of sauce.

Storage: Place airtight containers in the refrigerator for up to 1 week. To freeze, place freezer-safe containers in the freezer for up to 2 months. To defrost, refrigerate overnight. To reheat individual portions, microwave uncovered on high for about 2½ minutes.

TOBY'S TIP: Any of the following cuts of lean beef can be used in this recipe: eye or bottom round steaks or boneless chuck pot roast (shoulder, arm, or blade).

Per Serving (1 container): Calories: 476; Total Fat: 27g; Saturated Fat: 10g; Protein: 45g; Total Carbs: 10g; Fiber: 1g; Sugar: 3g; Sodium: 234mg

GARLIC-RUBBED STEAK WITH COUSCOUS AND CARROTS

MAKES 4 SERVINGS

PREP TIME: 15 minutes   **COOK TIME:** 20 minutes

You can enjoy lean cuts of beef, like top sirloin steak, in your healthy, well-balanced diet, even if you're trying to lose weight. Due to increased trimming practices over the last 30 years, there are more lean cuts of beef than ever before. While this recipe calls for cooking the steak on a grill pan or skillet, it is also terrific prepared on an outdoor grill.

Nonstick cooking spray

5 garlic cloves, minced

1 tablespoon olive oil

1 tablespoon Dijon mustard

1 teaspoon onion powder

½ teaspoon salt

¼ teaspoon freshly ground black pepper

1 (1¼ pounds) top sirloin steak

4 servings (2 cups) Parsleyed Whole-Wheat Couscous (page 144)

4 servings (2 cups) Lemon-Dill Carrots (page 149)

1. Preheat the oven to 400°F. Coat an ovenproof grill pan or skillet with cooking spray.

2. In a medium bowl, mix together the garlic, olive oil, mustard, onion powder, salt, and pepper. Add the steak and, using clean hands, rub the mixture onto both sides of the steak.

3. Heat the prepared grill pan over high heat. When the pan is hot, add the steak and cook for 2 minutes on each side. Place the pan in the oven and roast for 12 to 15 minutes until the steak reaches a minimum internal cooking temperature of 145°F.

4. Remove from the oven and transfer the steak to a cutting board. Allow to cool for 10 to 15 minutes before thinly slicing.

5. Into each of 4 containers, place ½ cup of Parsleyed Whole-Wheat Couscous, ½ cup of Lemon-Dill Carrots, and 4 ounces of steak.

Storage: Place airtight containers in the refrigerator for up to 1 week. To freeze, place freezer-safe containers in the freezer for up to 2 months. To defrost, refrigerate overnight. To reheat individual portions, microwave uncovered on high for 2 to 2½ minutes.

TOBY'S TIP: This rub is perfect for salmon or lean cuts of lamb like the leg, loin, or rack.

Per Serving (1 container): Calories: 564; Total Fat: 33g; Saturated Fat: 9g; Protein: 34g; Total Carbs: 33g; Fiber: 5g; Sugar: 6g; Sodium: 638mg

SLOW COOKER CHILI

MAKES 6 SERVINGS

PREP TIME: 15 minutes   COOK TIME: 4 hours

My family tends to have Sunday dinners together, but I also prepare some of our food for the week on Sundays. My answer to both: a hearty slow cooker dish.

1 tablespoon olive oil

1 pound lean (90% to 92%) ground beef

1 medium yellow onion, chopped

1 (15-ounce) can low-sodium black beans, rinsed and drained

1 (15-ounce) can low-sodium cannellini beans, rinsed and drained

1 (15-ounce) can low-sodium kidney beans, rinsed and drained

1 (4-ounce) can mild or hot green chiles

2 garlic cloves, minced

2 cups low-sodium beef or vegetable broth

1 (14.5-ounce) can no-salt-added diced tomatoes

1 (6-ounce) can tomato paste

2 tablespoons chili powder

1 tablespoon ground oregano

1 teaspoon ground cumin

1 teaspoon brown sugar

¼ teaspoon cayenne pepper

½ teaspoon salt

¼ teaspoon freshly ground black pepper

6 whole-grain dinner rolls

1. In a medium saucepan over medium heat, heat the oil. When the oil is shimmering, add the ground beef and cook, breaking up the meat into small pieces, until browned, about 8 minutes.

2. Put the cooked ground beef in the slow cooker. Add the onion, black beans, cannellini beans, kidney beans, chiles, garlic, broth, diced tomatoes, tomato paste, chili powder, oregano, cumin, brown sugar, cayenne, salt, and black pepper. Stir to thoroughly combine. Cover and cook on low for 4 hours.

3. Into each of 6 containers, place 1⅓ cups of chili.

4. Serve each portion with 1 dinner roll.

Storage: Place airtight containers (without the rolls) in the refrigerator for up to 1 week. To freeze, place freezer-safe containers (without the rolls) in the freezer for up to 2 months. To defrost, refrigerate overnight. To reheat individual portions, microwave uncovered on high for 2 to 2½ minutes. Alternatively, reheat the entire chili in a saucepan on the stove top. Bring the chili to a boil, then reduce the heat and simmer until heated through, 10 to 15 minutes. Serve with dinner rolls.

TOBY'S TIP: Add whole grains to the slow cooker—try farro, brown rice, or sorghum. Add the appropriate amount of extra liquid as listed on the label of the package.

Per Serving (1 container plus 1 roll): Calories: 504; Total Fat: 13g; Saturated Fat: 4g; Protein: 34g; Total Carbs: 65g; Fiber: 17g; Sugar: 10g; Sodium: 1,040mg

GRAINS & VEGETABLE SIDES

« Parsleyed Whole-Wheat Couscous (page 144)

HERBED QUINOA

MAKES 4 SERVINGS

PREP TIME: 15 minutes   **COOK TIME:** 15 minutes

Quinoa can add protein and whole grains to any dish. To add flavor to quinoa, there are several things you can do. First, instead of cooking the quinoa in water, opt for low-sodium broth, stock, or bone broth. Infuse even more flavor by tossing in some low-calorie herbs and lemon juice.

1 cup quinoa

2 cups low-sodium vegetable broth

⅓ cup chopped fresh parsley

⅓ cup chopped basil leaves

2 scallions (white and green parts), chopped

3 tablespoons olive oil

Juice of 1 lemon

¼ teaspoon salt

¼ teaspoon freshly ground black pepper

1.   In a medium saucepan over high heat, bring the quinoa and vegetable broth to a boil. Reduce the heat to low, cover, and simmer until all the liquid has been absorbed, 12 to 15 minutes. Remove from the heat and fluff the quinoa with a fork.

2.   In a medium bowl, whisk together the parsley, basil, scallions, oil, lemon juice, salt, and pepper. Add the quinoa and toss to combine.

3.   Into each of 4 containers, scoop ¾ cup of quinoa.

Storage: Place airtight containers in the refrigerator for up to 1 week. To freeze, place freezer-safe containers in the freezer for up to 2 months. To defrost, refrigerate overnight. Quinoa can be eaten cold or warm. To reheat individual servings, microwave uncovered on high for about 45 seconds.

TOBY'S TIP: To minimize food waste, use leftover fresh herbs you have from your garden or in your refrigerator. Herbs like cilantro and thyme can be used instead of or in addition to the herbs listed in this recipe.

Per Serving (¾ cup): Calories: 263; Total Fat: 13g; Saturated Fat: 2g; Protein: 7g; Total Carbs: 31g; Fiber: 4g; Sugar: 2g; Sodium: 224mg

FARRO WITH PEAS

PREP TIME: 15 minutes   COOK TIME: 40 minutes

This nutty whole grain dates back to ancient Rome. One cup of cooked farro contains 220 calories, 2 grams of fat, 8 grams of protein, and 5 grams of fiber. It also provides a boatload of antioxidant vitamins A and E, and minerals like iron and magnesium.

1¼ cups farro

3¾ cups low-sodium vegetable broth

2 tablespoons olive oil, divided

1 medium onion, chopped

1 garlic clove, minced

1 cup frozen peas, thawed

¼ cup chopped fresh dill

1 tablespoon red wine vinegar

¼ teaspoon salt

⅛ teaspoon freshly ground black pepper

1. In a medium pot, bring the farro and broth to a boil. Reduce the heat to medium-low and simmer until the farro is cooked through, about 30 minutes. Drain the excess liquid. Put the farro in a large bowl and set aside to slightly cool.

2. In a large saucepan, heat 1 tablespoon of oil. When the oil is shimmering, add the onion and garlic, and cook until the onion is soft and the garlic is fragrant, about 3 minutes. Add the peas, cover, and continue cooking until the peas are heated through, about 5 minutes.

3. Add the pea mixture to the farro and toss to combine. Add the remaining 1 tablespoon of oil, dill, vinegar, salt, and pepper, and toss to evenly coat.

4. Into each of 6 containers, scoop 1½ cups of farro.

Storage: Place airtight containers in the refrigerator for up to 1 week. To freeze, place freezer-safe containers in the freezer for up to 2 months. To defrost, refrigerate overnight. To reheat, microwave uncovered on high for 1 to 2 minutes. Alternatively, reheat the entire batch in a saucepan over medium heat for 5 to 8 minutes. Add a splash of liquid if reheating on the stove top.

TOBY'S TIP: For a similar dish using a nutty whole grain, swap the farro for brown rice or barley.

Per Serving (1 container): Calories: 265; Total Fat: 8g; Saturated Fat: 1g; Protein: 8g; Total Carbs: 38g; Fiber: 8g; Sugar: 4g; Sodium: 213mg

BROWN RICE WITH LENTILS

MAKES 6 SERVINGS

PREP TIME: 10 minutes   **COOK TIME:** 50 minutes

This spin on rice and beans ups the nutrients with lentils. Lentils, an underappreciated legume, have a sturdier texture and more peppery flavor than beans, peas, or other legumes. These babies provide both healthy protein and complex carbohydrates, and they're full of fiber to keep you satisfied longer. The soluble fiber found in legumes has also been shown to help lower cholesterol.

2 cups low-sodium vegetable broth or water

1 cup long-grain brown rice

1 tablespoon olive oil

1 medium onion, chopped

2 garlic cloves, minced

2 bay leaves

1 (15-ounce) can brown lentils, rinsed and drained

¼ teaspoon salt

¼ teaspoon freshly ground black pepper

1.   In a medium pot over high heat, bring the broth to a boil. Stir in the brown rice and reduce the heat to medium-low. Cover and simmer, stirring occasionally, until the rice is tender, about 40 minutes. Drain any excess water. Transfer the rice to a large bowl, fluff with a fork, and allow to cool slightly.

2.   In a medium saucepan over medium heat, heat the oil until it shimmers. Add the onion, garlic, and bay leaves and cook until the onion is translucent, about 3 minutes. Add the lentils and cook until heated through, about 5 minutes. Set the saucepan aside and allow to slightly cool. Remove and discard the bay leaves.

3.   Stir the onion-lentil mixture into the rice and toss to combine. Sprinkle with the salt and pepper and stir to incorporate.

4.   Into each of 6 containers, scoop ¾ cup of rice.

Storage: Place airtight containers in the refrigerator for up to 1 week. To freeze, place freezer-safe containers in the freezer for up to 2 months. To defrost, refrigerate overnight. To reheat, microwave uncovered on high for 1 to 2 minutes.

TOBY'S TIP: Swap the lentils for black beans for a quick and easy rice and beans dish.

Per Serving (¾ cup): Calories: 204; Total Fat: 4g; Saturated Fat: 0g; Protein: 7g; Total Carbs: 37g; Fiber: 8g; Sugar: 3g; Sodium: 228mg

MOROCCAN-STYLE SORGHUM WITH CARROTS

MAKES 6 SERVINGS

PREP TIME: 15 minutes   COOK TIME: 25 minutes

Sorghum is an ancient grain thought to have originated in Africa. Over the past few years, it has become more popular in the United States, where you can now find it on the menu at popular restaurants. A quarter cup of dry sorghum provides 158 calories, 5 grams of protein, 35 grams of carbs, and 3 grams of fiber. It's also a good source of iron, providing 12 percent of the recommended daily amount.

1¼ cups pearled sorghum

3¾ cups low-sodium vegetable broth

3 medium carrots, peeled and shredded

3 tablespoons olive oil

Juice of ½ lemon (about 1 tablespoon)

1 tablespoon fennel seeds

1 teaspoon ground cumin

1 teaspoon ground coriander

¼ teaspoon salt

⅛ teaspoon freshly ground black pepper

1. In a medium saucepan, bring the sorghum and broth to a boil. Reduce the heat, cover, and simmer, stirring occasionally, until the sorghum becomes puffed and softens, about 25 minutes. Remove the sorghum from the heat.

2. Add the shredded carrots and toss until evenly distributed.

3. In a small bowl, whisk together the oil, lemon juice, fennel, cumin, coriander, salt, and pepper. Drizzle over the sorghum and toss to evenly coat.

4. Into each of 6 containers, scoop ¾ cup of sorghum.

Storage: Place airtight containers in the refrigerator for up to 1 week. To freeze, place freezer-safe containers in the freezer for up to 2 months. To defrost, refrigerate overnight. To reheat, microwave uncovered on high for 1 to 2 minutes. Alternatively, reheat the entire batch in a saucepan over medium heat for 5 to 8 minutes until heated through. Add a splash of liquid if reheating on the stove top.

TOBY'S TIP: Sorghum is available at specialty stores or online. Pearled sorghum is quicker to cook than regular sorghum (25 minutes versus 45 minutes). You can also swap the sorghum for brown rice, farro, or barley.

Per Serving (¾ cup): Calories: 222; Total Fat: 7g; Saturated Fat: 1g; Protein: 4g; Total Carbs: 36g; Fiber: 3g; Sugar: 3g; Sodium: 208mg

PARSLEYED WHOLE-WHEAT COUSCOUS

MAKES 8 SERVINGS

PREP TIME: 10 minutes   COOK TIME: 5 minutes

There are various types of couscous including Moroccan, Israeli, and Lebanese. The smallest, Moroccan (used in this recipe), is about three times the size of cornmeal and cooks up in about five minutes. One cup of cooked couscous contains 176 calories, 36 grams of carbohydrates, 2 grams of fiber, and 6 grams of protein, with no sugar or fat. It also contains 67 percent of your recommended daily selenium. Whole-wheat couscous has 5 to 6 grams of fiber per serving and is also available in many markets.

2 cups low-sodium vegetable or chicken broth

1 cup chopped fresh parsley, reserving about ¼ cup stems

Juice and rind of 1 lemon

3 tablespoons olive oil, divided

1¼ cups whole-wheat couscous

¼ teaspoon salt

⅛ teaspoon freshly ground black pepper

1.   In a medium saucepan, bring the broth, parsley stems, lemon rind, and 1 tablespoon of olive oil to a boil. Stir in the couscous and cover. Remove from the heat and let stand for 5 minutes. Uncover and fluff the couscous with a fork. Remove and discard the parsley stems and lemon rind.

2.   Put the couscous in a medium bowl. Add the chopped parsley, lemon juice, remaining 2 tablespoons of oil, salt, and pepper, and toss to combine.

3.   Into each of 8 containers, scoop ½ cup of couscous.

Storage: Place airtight containers in the refrigerator for up to 7 days. Couscous can be eaten cold or warm. To reheat, microwave uncovered on high for about 30 seconds.

TOBY'S TIP: For a change of pace, try Israeli (or pearled) couscous, which is larger than traditional couscous. It has a rounder shape (more like a peppercorn) and takes longer to cook. Follow the package directions for the appropriate cooking time.

Per Serving (½ cup): Calories: 151; Total Fat: 6g; Saturated Fat: 1g; Protein: 4g; Total Carbs: 24g; Fiber: 3g; Sugar: 1g; Sodium: 113mg

CAULIFLOWER RICE WITH MUSHROOMS

MAKES 6 SERVINGS

PREP TIME: 15 minutes   COOK TIME: 20 minutes

Cauliflower rice is a perfect substitute for rice, and it cooks up quickly. Riced cauliflower provides 80 calories and 5 grams of fat per cup and has a pretty mild flavor. You can find it in the freezer section of your grocery store, or make your own (see Toby's Tip).

2 tablespoons olive oil, divided

1 medium onion, chopped

1 (8-ounce) container baby bella (cremini) mushrooms, chopped

1 cup low-sodium vegetable or chicken broth

2 (10-ounce) bags frozen riced cauliflower

½ teaspoon salt

¼ teaspoon freshly ground black pepper

1. In a medium saucepan over medium heat, heat 1 tablespoon of olive oil. When the oil is shimmering, add the onion and cook until translucent, about 3 minutes.

2. Add the mushrooms and continue cooking until they soften, about 5 minutes.

3. Add the vegetable or chicken broth and bring the mixture to a boil.

4. Add the riced cauliflower and stir to incorporate. Reduce the heat to medium-low, cover, and cook until the cauliflower is heated through, about 10 minutes.

5. Add the remaining 1 tablespoon of oil, salt, and pepper, and toss to combine.

6. Into each of 6 containers, scoop ¾ cup of cauliflower.

Storage: Place airtight containers in the refrigerator for up to 1 week. To freeze, place freezer-safe containers in the freezer for up to 2 months. To defrost, refrigerate overnight. To reheat, microwave uncovered on high for 1 to 2 minutes. Alternatively, reheat the entire batch in a saucepan over medium heat for about 5 to 8 minutes until heated through. Add a splash of liquid if reheating on the stove top.

TOBY'S TIP: Make your own riced cauliflower by placing cauliflower florets in a blender and pulsing until it turns into a fine rice.

Per Serving (¾ cup): Calories: 81; Total Fat: 5g; Saturated Fat: 1g; Protein: 4g; Total Carbs: 8g; Fiber: 3g; Sugar: 4g; Sodium: 300mg

ZUCCHINI NOODLES WITH LEMON VINAIGRETTE

MAKES 4 SERVINGS

PREP TIME: 15 minutes

I'm not into purchasing special equipment for my kitchen. There's plenty I can do with just a few basic kitchen tools. But once I gave the spiralizer a whirl (literally!), I discovered it was so easy to use and to clean—and so much cheaper than buying spiralized foods. You can spiralize most fruits and vegetables to create long, perfect noodles. These zucchini noodles are a creative way to add more veggies to your diet and keep your total daily carbs in check.

Juice and zest of 1 lemon

2 tablespoons extra-virgin olive oil

1 teaspoon honey

1 teaspoon Dijon mustard

¼ teaspoon salt

⅛ teaspoon freshly ground black pepper

3 medium zucchini, or 6 cups precut zucchini noodles

SPECIAL EQUIPMENT

Spiralizer

1. In a large bowl, whisk together the lemon juice and zest, olive oil, honey, Dijon mustard, salt, and pepper.

2. Using a spiralizer, make zucchini noodles and add to the bowl with the lemon vinaigrette. Toss to combine.

3. Into each of 4 containers, place 1½ cups noodles.

Storage: Place airtight containers in the refrigerator for up to 3 days.

TOBY'S TIP: These noodles can be eaten raw or cooked. To blanch them, put the noodles in boiling water for 3 to 4 minutes. Prepare a large bowl of ice (no water). Use tongs to quickly remove the cooked noodles and place them on top of the ice. This quick cooking method ensures the noodles remain firm and retain their full nutrients.

Per Serving (1½ cups): Calories: 95; Total Fat: 8g; Saturated Fat: 1g; Protein: 2g; Total Carbs: 7g; Fiber: 2g; Sugar: 5g; Sodium: 191mg

ROASTED BROCCOLI WITH SHALLOTS

MAKES 4 SERVINGS

PREP TIME: 15 minutes   **COOK TIME:** 15 minutes

Broccoli is a simple, inexpensive vegetable that's perfect for meal prep. The green veggie is also part of the cruciferous (cabbage) family, whose members contain isothiocyanates and indoles shown to help lower the risk of certain forms of cancer, including breast, lung, colorectal, and prostate.

1 pound broccoli crowns, cut into bite-size florets

1 shallot, chopped

¼ cup olive oil

¼ teaspoon salt

¼ teaspoon freshly ground black pepper

⅛ teaspoon red pepper flakes

1.   Preheat the oven to 450°F. Line a baking sheet with parchment paper or aluminum foil.

2.   In a large bowl, toss the broccoli florets and shallot together to combine.

3.   In a small bowl, whisk together the oil, salt, black pepper, and red pepper flakes. Pour the oil mixture over the broccoli, tossing to evenly coat.

4.   Spread the broccoli on the prepared baking sheet in a single layer. Bake for 10 to 12 minutes until the broccoli is slightly browned.

5.   Into each of 4 containers, place 1 cup of broccoli.

Storage: Place airtight containers in the refrigerator for up to 1 week. To freeze, place freezer-safe containers in the freezer for up to 2 months. To defrost, refrigerate overnight. To reheat, microwave uncovered on high for 45 seconds to 1 minute.

TOBY'S TIP: Swap the shallot for yellow onion, or make a garlic-roasted broccoli instead using 4 or 5 thinly sliced garlic cloves.

Per Serving (about 1 cup): Calories: 159; Total Fat: 14g; Saturated Fat: 2g; Protein: 4g; Total Carbs: 8g; Fiber: 0g; Sugar: 1g; Sodium: 179mg

LEMON-DILL CARROTS

MAKES 6 SERVINGS

PREP TIME: 10 minutes   COOK TIME: 10 minutes

Carrots are one of the best sources of beta-carotene around. That's the antioxidant form of vitamin A, which helps protect the body from heart disease and certain forms of cancer, and helps maintain good eyesight. Carrots also provide a healthy dose of fiber, vitamin C, vitamin K, and potassium.

1 (1-pound) bag baby carrots

¼ cup olive oil

¼ cup chopped fresh dill

Juice and zest of 1 lemon

1 teaspoon white wine vinegar

1 teaspoon honey

¼ teaspoon salt

¼ teaspoon freshly ground black pepper

1. Pour ½ cup of water into a medium pot fitted with a steamer basket, and bring to a boil over high heat. Add the carrots, cover, and reduce the heat to medium. Cook until tender, 10 minutes.

2. Meanwhile, in a large bowl, whisk together the oil, dill, lemon juice and zest, vinegar, honey, salt, and pepper. When cooked, add the warm carrots and toss to combine.

3. Into each of 4 containers, place ½ cup of carrots.

Storage: Place airtight containers in the refrigerator for up to 1 week. To freeze, place freezer-safe containers in the freezer for up to 2 months. To defrost, refrigerate overnight. To reheat, microwave uncovered on high for 1 minute.

TOBY'S TIP: When choosing fresh dill, choose bunches that are aromatic, bright green, and firm. Store in the refrigerator wrapped in a paper towel for 2 to 3 days. Wash and dry well just before using.

Per Serving (about ½ cup): Calories: 111; Total Fat: 9g; Saturated Fat: 1g; Protein: 1g; Total Carbs: 8g; Fiber: 2g; Sugar: 5g; Sodium: 158mg

SNACKS

◀◀ Baked Almond Cherry Bars (page 161)

SIMPLE HUMMUS WITH VEGETABLES

MAKES 6 SERVINGS

PREP TIME: 15 minutes

Chickpeas are nutrient-packed legumes that can be part of any healthy eating plan. They have a nice combination of carbs, protein, and healthy fat. A half-cup (cooked or canned) provides 143 calories, 6 grams of protein, 26 grams of carbs, and just 1.3 grams of fat. They're an excellent source of fiber, vitamin B6, and folate, and provide smaller amounts of iron, magnesium, potassium, zinc, and selenium.

1 (15-ounce) can low-sodium chickpeas, rinsed and drained

1 garlic clove, minced

2 tablespoons tahini

Juice of 2 lemons (about ¼ cup)

½ teaspoon salt

¼ teaspoon freshly ground black pepper

¼ cup extra-virgin olive oil

2 to 4 tablespoons water

10 celery stalks, washed, trimmed, and cut in half

6 medium carrots, peeled, halved lengthwise, and cut in half

6 radishes, washed, trimmed, and halved

1. In a food processor or blender, process the chickpeas, garlic, tahini, lemon juice, salt, and pepper together until well combined. With the machine running, slowly drizzle in the olive oil and water, and continue processing until well incorporated and creamy. If you want a thinner consistency, add more water, 1 tablespoon at a time.

2. Into each of 6 resealable containers or mason jars, spoon ¼ cup hummus and divide the vegetables evenly.

Storage: Place airtight containers in the refrigerator for up to 5 days.

TOBY'S TIP: Flavor your hummus by adding a fun ingredient to your blender, like a handful of parsley, 1 to 2 teaspoons of Sriracha, or a few roasted red peppers.

Per Serving (1 container): Calories: 242; Total Fat: 14g; Saturated Fat: 2g; Protein: 7g; Total Carbs: 25g; Fiber: 7g; Sugar: 7g; Sodium: 451mg

TO-GO PEANUT BUTTER– VEGGIE JARS

MAKES 5 SERVINGS

PREP TIME: 10 minutes

Keep these easy grabs on hand! Filled with protein and unsaturated healthy fat that takes longer to digest, peanut butter is the perfect snack to keep you satisfied until your next meal.

7½ tablespoons smooth or chunky peanut or almond butter, divided

10 celery stalks, washed, trimmed, and cut in half

5 medium carrots, peeled, halved lengthwise, and cut in half

10 pretzel rods, preferably whole-grain, broken in half

1.   Into the bottom of each of 5 mason jars, spoon 1½ tablespoons of peanut butter.

2.   Evenly divide the vegetables and place them "standing up" in the jar. Add 2 pretzel rod halves to each jar.

Storage: Place covered jars in the refrigerator for up to 5 days. Allow to sit at room temperature for about 30 minutes before eating.

TOBY'S TIP: Switch the peanut butter for almond butter, sunflower seed butter, soy nut butter, walnut butter, or cashew butter.

Per Serving (1 jar): Calories: 252; Total Fat: 13g; Saturated Fat: 2g; Protein: 8g; Total Carbs: 29g; Fiber: 5g; Sugar: 7g; Sodium: 627mg

SPICY EDAMAME

PREP TIME: 5 minutes   COOK TIME: 5 minutes

When I get a salty craving, I turn to edamame. Unlike potato chips that leave me feeling hungry again rather quickly, baby soybeans are brimming with protein, which helps fill me up. If this is your first time trying edamame, you'll want to know that only the beans are eaten, not the pod—just bite the pod to release the edible beans. This recipe has you prep 5 containers for the week, and makes about 3 extra servings to snack on or share.

2 (14-ounce) packages frozen edamame in the shell (unsalted)

2 tablespoons low-sodium soy sauce

1 tablespoon Sriracha

2 teaspoons toasted sesame oil

1. Fill a large pot three-quarters full with water and bring to a boil. Add the edamame and cook until heated through, about 5 minutes. Drain, and place the edamame in a large bowl. Set aside to cool.

2. In a small bowl, whisk together the soy sauce, Sriracha, and sesame oil. Pour the sauce over the edamame and toss to evenly coat.

3. Into each of 5 containers, scoop 1½ cups of edamame.

Storage: Place airtight containers in the refrigerator for up to 1 week. To reheat, microwave uncovered on high for 1 minute. You can also enjoy the edamame cold.

TOBY'S TIP: Look for edamame in the pod in the frozen section of the supermarket. It's usually near the vegetable or "healthy" section.

Per Serving (1½ cups): Calories: 154; Total Fat: 7g; Saturated Fat: 1g; Protein: 12g; Total Carbs: 11g; Fiber: 4g; Sugar: 3g; Sodium: 147mg

PARMESAN POPCORN

MAKES 5 SERVINGS

PREP TIME: 10 minutes   COOK TIME: 5 minutes

Popcorn is a whole grain, and some folks are surprised to learn that it's a nutritious food if prepared in a healthy manner. One cup of air-popped popcorn has 31 calories, 5 percent of the recommended daily amount of fiber, and small amounts of several vitamins and minerals. Topped with a sprinkle of Parmesan cheese, this movie-time favorite makes for a deliciously healthy snack.

3 tablespoons olive oil

½ cup popcorn kernels

Nonstick cooking spray

½ cup grated
   Parmesan cheese

1.   In a large pot over medium-low heat, heat the olive oil. Add 3 popcorn kernels, and when one of the kernels pops, add the rest. Cover and shake the pot occasionally to prevent burning. Once fully popped, transfer the popcorn to a large bowl. Alternatively, use a popcorn maker to air-pop the popcorn.

2.   Spray the popcorn with cooking spray and sprinkle with the Parmesan. Use clean hands to toss the popcorn, mixing it thoroughly.

3.   Into each of 5 resealable plastic bags or containers, pour 2¾ cups of popcorn.

Storage: Place sealed bags in the refrigerator for up to 1 week. Remove the bag at least 30 minutes before eating, so the popcorn warms to room temperature.

TOBY'S TIP: The cooking spray is used to help the spices or cheese stick to the popcorn. That said, experiment with different spices!

Per Serving (1 container): Calories: 179; Total Fat: 12g; Saturated Fat: 3g; Protein: 6g; Total Carbs: 16g; Fiber: 3g; Sugar: 0g; Sodium: 153mg

NUTTY TRAIL MIX

MAKES 5 SERVINGS

PREP TIME: 5 minutes

This quick and easy snack can be tweaked to suit your taste buds. Choose your favorite nuts, dried fruit, and chocolate chips, and complement them with something crunchy. The nuts provide healthy fat, protein, and a variety of vitamins and minerals, while the dried fruit provides a boatload of antioxidants.

¼ cup unsalted cashews

¼ cup unsalted roasted peanuts

¼ cup dried cranberries

¼ cup dark chocolate chips

½ cup salted pretzels, preferably whole-wheat

1. In a medium bowl, toss the cashews, peanuts, cranberries, chocolate chips, and pretzels together to combine.

2. Into each of 5 resealable plastic bags or containers, place ⅓ cup of trail mix.

Storage: Store airtight bags at room temperature for up to 1 month.

TOBY'S TIP: Trail mix can rack up the calories quickly, so it's important to keep a close eye on portions.

Per Serving (⅓ cup): Calories: 209; Total Fat: 11g; Saturated Fat: 3g; Protein: 4g; Total Carbs: 25g; Fiber: 2g; Sugar: 11g; Sodium: 154mg

PEANUT BUTTER–CHOCOLATE BITES

MAKES 12 BITES

PREP TIME: 15 minutes

Unsweetened cocoa powder is a low-calorie option to add chocolate to a recipe. One tablespoon contains 20 calories, 3 grams of carbs, and 1 gram of protein, and is free of added sugar. It's also a good source of iron, providing 10 percent of your recommended daily needs. As cocoa powder is unsweetened, you'll want to add a touch of sweetness to enhance the flavor.

¾ cup natural peanut butter

¼ cup quick-cooking oats

¼ cup 100% pure maple syrup

2 tablespoons unsweetened cocoa powder

1 teaspoon vanilla extract

¼ cup dark chocolate chips

1. In a blender, process the peanut butter, oats, maple syrup, cocoa powder, and vanilla together until smooth.

2. Scrape the batter into a medium bowl, and fold in the chocolate chips.

3. Spoon out a tablespoon of batter. Using clean hands, roll it into a 2-inch ball. Repeat with the remaining batter.

Storage: Place in one or more airtight containers in the refrigerator, allowing the bites to set for at least 15 minutes. Store for up to 1 week.

TOBY'S TIP: Play around with your natural sweeteners. Swap the maple syrup for honey, unsulfured molasses, or agave.

Per Serving (1 bite): Calories: 147; Total Fat: 10g; Saturated Fat: 3g; Protein: 4g; Total Carbs: 13g; Fiber: 2g; Sugar: 8g; Sodium: 77mg

CARROT-ZUCCHINI MINI MUFFINS

MAKES 36 MINI MUFFINS

PREP TIME: 15 minutes   **COOK TIME:** 20 minutes

The shredded carrot and zucchini displace some of the flour required in traditional muffin recipes. This also helps remove some of the calories, making these a lower-calorie choice.

Nonstick cooking spray

1 cup unbleached all-purpose flour

1 teaspoon ground cinnamon

½ teaspoon baking powder

¼ teaspoon baking soda

¼ cup (½ stick) unsalted butter, melted and cooled

½ cup unsweetened applesauce

½ cup packed light brown sugar

1 teaspoon vanilla extract

2 large eggs, beaten

1 large zucchini, shredded

2 medium carrots, peeled and shredded

½ cup golden raisins

1. Preheat the oven to 350°F. Coat two 24-count mini muffin tins with cooking spray.

2. In a medium bowl, sift together the flour, cinnamon, baking powder, and baking soda.

3. In a large bowl, whisk together the melted butter, apple-sauce, brown sugar, vanilla, and eggs.

4. Gradually stir the dry mixture into the wet until just combined, being careful to not overmix.

5. Fold in the zucchini, carrots, and raisins until evenly distributed.

6. Spoon 2 tablespoons of batter into each of 36 mini muffin cups. Tap the pan a few times on the counter to release any air bubbles. Bake for 15 to 20 minutes until a toothpick inserted in the center of a mini muffin comes out clean.

7. Remove from the oven and allow to cool for 10 minutes. Transfer the mini muffins to a wire rack and let cool completely.

Storage: Store in airtight containers at room temperature for up to 5 days. To freeze, place freezer-safe containers in the freezer for up to 2 months. To defrost, let muffins sit at room temperature. Muffins can be reheated in a toaster oven or in a 350°F oven for 5 minutes.

Per Serving (4 mini muffins): Calories: 196; Total Fat: 6g; Saturated Fat: 4g; Protein: 4g; Total Carbs: 32g; Fiber: 2g; Sugar: 20g; Sodium: 83mg

SUNFLOWER POWER BITES

MAKES 12 BITES

PREP TIME: 15 minutes

As they say, good things come in small packages. One quarter cup of shelled sunflower seeds contains 67 calories, 2 grams of fat, 2 grams of protein, and 1 gram of fiber. It also provides an abundance of vitamins and minerals, including the antioxidant vitamin E, numerous B vitamins, iron, phosphorus, and selenium. In these bites, you'll get a double dose of nutrients from both the sunflower seeds and the sunflower seed butter.

¾ cup quick-cooking oats

¼ cup toasted wheat germ

½ cup sunflower seed butter

⅓ cup 100% pure maple syrup

1 teaspoon vanilla extract

½ teaspoon ground cinnamon

⅛ teaspoon salt

¼ cup unsalted sunflower seeds

¼ cup golden raisins

1.   In a blender, process the oats, wheat germ, sunflower seed butter, maple syrup, vanilla, cinnamon, and salt until smooth.

2.   Scrape the batter into a medium bowl, and fold in the sunflower seeds and raisins.

3.   Spoon out a tablespoon of batter. Using clean hands, roll it into a 2-inch ball. Repeat with the remaining batter.

Storage: Place in one or more airtight containers in the refrigerator, allowing the bites to set for at least 15 minutes. Store for up to 1 week.

TOBY'S TIP: You can find sunflower seed butter in the peanut butter aisle, specialty stores, or online. You can also swap it for a mild nut butter such as almond.

Per Serving (1 bite): Calories: 141; Total Fat: 8g; Saturated Fat: 1g; Protein: 4g; Total Carbs: 16g; Fiber: 2g; Sugar: 9g; Sodium: 26mg

BAKED ALMOND CHERRY BARS | MAKES 16 BARS

PREP TIME: 15 minutes   COOK TIME: 30 minutes

To feel great, it's important to have snacks filled with good-for-you ingredients. These babies provide nutrients from four food groups, including whole grains, protein, dairy, and fruit. The calories are 121 per bar, but you're getting a full array of nutrients in every delicious bite!

½ cup quinoa

1 ½ cups gluten-free quick-cooking oats

½ cup almonds, chopped

½ cup dried tart cherries

1 cup low-fat (1%) milk

¼ cup 100% pure maple syrup

1 teaspoon vanilla extract

¼ cup cherry preserves

1. Preheat the oven to 350°F. Line an 8-by-8-inch baking dish with parchment paper.

2. Pour the quinoa into a blender and blend until smooth.

3. In a medium bowl, mix together the blended quinoa, oats, almonds, cherries, milk, maple syrup, and vanilla. Pour the mixture into the prepared baking dish. Use a spatula or the back of a spoon to evenly distribute the mixture.

4. Top with the cherry preserves, and use a spatula or the back of a spoon to evenly spread the preserves over the top.

5. Bake for about 30 minutes until the edges are slightly browned. Remove from the oven and allow to cool for 15 minutes before slicing into 12 bars.

6. Wrap the bars in plastic wrap or place in a resealable container.

Storage: Store wrapped or in an airtight container at room temperature for up to 1 week.

TOBY'S TIP: Oats are naturally gluten-free; however, some oats are manufactured in facilities with wheat and other gluten-filled foods. If it's an issue, read the label to make sure your oats are gluten-free.

Per Serving (1 bar): Calories: 121; Total Fat: 3g; Saturated Fat: 0g; Protein: 3g; Total Carbs: 21g; Fiber: 2g; Sugar: 11g; Sodium: 13mg

DEVILED EGGS WITH SPICY BLACK BEAN STUFFING

MAKES 5 SERVINGS

PREP TIME: 15 minutes   **COOK TIME:** 5 minutes

Eggs are a fantastic snack on their own, but making a deviled version takes them to a whole new level. The black bean stuffing complements the egg white by adding a ton of flavor as well as protein, fiber, thiamin, folate, iron, magnesium, and potassium. It's truly a snack that gets the job done by adding nutrients that you may not otherwise get enough of throughout the day.

10 large eggs

1 (15-ounce can) low-sodium black beans, rinsed and drained

1 (4-ounce) can diced green chiles, mild or spicy

1 tablespoon tomato paste

1 teaspoon ground cumin

1 teaspoon chili powder

¼ teaspoon smoked paprika

¼ teaspoon salt

⅛ teaspoon cayenne pepper

1.   Hard-boil the eggs by placing them in a medium pot and covering them with water. Over high heat, bring the water to a boil. Cook the eggs for 3 minutes, then remove the pot from the heat, cover, and let the eggs stand for 15 minutes. Drain the water and place the eggs in a bowl of ice until completely cool, about 10 minutes. Peel the eggs and slice lengthwise. Remove the yolks and reserve for another purpose (see Toby's Tip).

2.   In a blender, process the black beans, chiles, tomato paste, cumin, chili powder, paprika, salt, and cayenne together until smooth.

3.   Spoon 1 tablespoon of black bean mixture into each of the 20 egg white halves.

4.   Into each of 5 containers, place 4 stuffed egg halves.

Storage: Place airtight containers in the refrigerator for up to 1 week.

TOBY'S TIP: Swap the black beans for kidney or pinto beans. And use those leftover yolks for an egg salad!

Per Serving (4 stuffed egg halves): Calories: 123; Total Fat: 1g; Saturated Fat: 0g; Protein: 13g; Total Carbs: 17g; Fiber: 7g; Sugar: 1g; Sodium: 450mg

SNACK-SIZE BURRITO JARS

MAKES 5 SERVINGS

PREP TIME: 15 minutes   COOK TIME: 15 minutes

I crave Mexican fare—it's one of my favorite cuisines, hands down. When I'm really on a Mexican food kick, I'll make these snack jars so I can enjoy them as a snack. With beans, chicken, quinoa, and an array of veggies, it's well balanced and keeps me extremely satisfied until my next meal.

½ cup quinoa

1 cup low-sodium vegetable or chicken broth

1 (15-ounce) can low-sodium black beans, drained and rinsed

1 medium red bell pepper, chopped

2 plum tomatoes, chopped

1 jalapeño pepper, ribbed, seeded, and finely diced

¼ cup chopped fresh cilantro

2 tablespoons olive oil

Juice of 1 lime

¼ teaspoon salt

⅛ teaspoon freshly ground black pepper

4 ounces leftover grilled skinless, boneless chicken breast, cut into chunks

5 tablespoons shredded Pepper Jack cheese, divided

1.   In a medium saucepan over high heat, bring the quinoa and broth to a boil. Reduce the heat to low, cover, and simmer until all the liquid has been absorbed, 12 to 15 minutes. Remove from the heat and fluff the quinoa with a fork.

2.   In a medium bowl, combine the black beans, bell pepper, tomatoes, jalapeño, cilantro, oil, lime juice, salt, and black pepper. Toss to evenly coat.

3.   In each of 5 mini glass jars (approximately 8 ounces each), layer 3 tablespoons of quinoa, about 2 tablespoons of chicken, and finally ⅔ cup of bean mixture. Sprinkle each jar with 1 tablespoon of shredded cheese.

Storage: Place covered jars in the refrigerator for up to 5 days. Enjoy cold.

TOBY'S TIP: Swap the grilled chicken for leftover steak or turkey, or keep it out completely for a vegetarian version.

Per Serving (1 jar): Calories: 251; Total Fat: 9g; Saturated Fat: 3g; Protein: 16g; Total Carbs: 27g; Fiber: 8g; Sugar: 2g; Sodium: 328mg

Measurement Conversion Tables

Volume Equivalents (Liquid)

US STANDARD	US STANDARD (OUNCES)	METRIC (APPROXIMATE)
2 TABLESPOONS	1 FL. OZ.	30 ML
¼ CUP	2 FL. OZ.	60 ML
½ CUP	4 FL. OZ.	120 ML
1 CUP	8 FL. OZ.	240 ML
1½ CUPS	12 FL. OZ.	355 ML
2 CUPS OR 1 PINT	16 FL. OZ.	475 ML
4 CUPS OR 1 QUART	32 FL. OZ.	1 L
1 GALLON	128 FL. OZ.	4 L

Oven Temperatures

FAHRENHEIT (F)	CELSIUS (C) (APPROXIMATE)
250°F	120°C
300°F	150°C
325°F	165°C
350°F	180°C
375°F	190°C
400°F	200°C
425°F	220°C
450°F	230°C

Volume Equivalents (Dry)

US STANDARD	METRIC (APPROXIMATE)
⅛ TEASPOON	0.5 ML
¼ TEASPOON	1 ML
½ TEASPOON	2 ML
¾ TEASPOON	4 ML
1 TEASPOON	5 ML
1 TABLESPOON	15 ML
¼ CUP	59 ML
⅓ CUP	79 ML
½ CUP	118 ML
⅔ CUP	156 ML
¾ CUP	177 ML
1 CUP	235 ML
2 CUPS OR 1 PINT	475 ML
3 CUPS	700 ML
4 CUPS OR 1 QUART	1 L
½ GALLON	2 L
1 GALLON	4 L

Weight Equivalents

US STANDARD	METRIC (APPROXIMATE)
½ OUNCE	15 GRAMS
1 OUNCE	30 GRAMS
2 OUNCES	60 GRAMS
4 OUNCES	115 GRAMS
8 OUNCES	225 GRAMS
12 OUNCES	340 GRAMS
16 OUNCES OR 1 POUND	455 GRAMS

Recipe Index

Index

Acknowledgments

There are many people I want to thank for making this cookbook possible. First and foremost, thank you to my three children, Schoen, Ellena, and Micah, for hanging in during this cookbook writing experience. I know my schedule has been insane, but you have all been so supportive. I love you. Micah, thank you for being my helper in the kitchen, and I know you picked up some recipe development skills at the age of 10 years old. Ellena and Schoen, thank you for being my special taste testers and eating all the recipes I cook. All three of you are the forces that drive everything I do and have taught me the true meaning of life and love. Thank you to my loving boyfriend and best friend Shaun Swersky, who is always available to taste-test recipes. You have been so supportive throughout this entire process. Thank you as always to my parents, Henry and Zipporah Oksman, for guiding me throughout life to follow my dreams.

A huge thank-you to my teammate, fellow registered dietitian, and sister-in-law Gena Seraita, MS, RD, for helping me from brainstorming to recipe testing, and my assistant Cristiane Camargo for helping me with anything and everything that needed to get done.

Last but certainly not least, thank you to Sally Ekus, Jaimee Constantine, and Sara Pokorny from The Lisa Ekus Group for your support and kindness throughout this process. Many thanks to my editor, Stacy Wagner-Kinnear, and the dedicated and hardworking team at Callisto Media for working diligently to bring this amazing project to life.

About the Author

TOBY AMIDOR, MS, RD, CDN, a veteran in the food and nutrition industry with close to 20 years of experience, is a leading dietitian and recipe developer who believes that healthy and wholesome food can also be appetizing and delicious.

Toby is the founder of Toby Amidor Nutrition, where she provides nutrition and food safety consulting services for individuals, restaurants, and food brands. For 10 years, she has been the nutrition expert for *FoodNetwork.com* and founding contributor to its *Healthy Eats* blog. She is a regular contributor to *U.S. News & World Report Eat + Run* blog and *MensFitness.com*, and she has her own "Ask the Expert" column in *Today's Dietitian* magazine. She has been quoted in publications like *FoxNews.com, Self.com, Oxygen Magazine, Dr. Oz The Good Life, Mic.com, Reader's Digest, Shape.com, Women's Health, Redbook, Men's Journal, Huffington Post, Everyday Health*, and more. Toby has also appeared on television, including *The Dr. Oz Show, Coffee with America,* Fox 5 NY's *Good Day Street Talk*, and *San Antonio Live.* For the past nine years, she has been an adjunct professor at Teachers College, Columbia University, and is currently an adjunct at CUNY Hunter College School of Urban Public Health in New York City. Previously, she was a consultant on Bobby Deen's cooking show, *Not My Mama's Meals.*

Toby is the *Wall Street Journal*–bestselling cookbook author of *The Greek Yogurt Kitchen: More Than 130 Delicious, Healthy Recipes for Every Meal of the Day* (Grand Central Publishing, 2014), *The Healthy Meal Prep Cookbook: Easy and Wholesome Meals to Cook, Prep, Grab, and Go* (Rockridge Press, 2017), and *The Easy 5-Ingredient Cookbook: Simple Recipes to Make Healthy Eating Delicious* (Rockridge Press, 2018).

Toby trained as a clinical dietitian at New York University. Through ongoing consulting and faculty positions, she has established herself as one of the top experts in culinary nutrition, food safety, and nutrition communication.